I0480223

THE 23 IMMUTABLE LAWS OF SELLING

Revealed!

- Timeless Secrets on How to Sell More

- Proven Tactics on How to Eliminate Competitors

- Dirty Truths about Acquiring Customers

The ultimate salesman handbook that teaches the art and science of selling with fool-proof formulae that are the working tools of successful sales professionals.

© 2021 Joshua Riches

All rights reserved. No portion of this book may be reproduced, stored in a retrieval system, or transmitted in any form or by any means - electronic, mechanical, photocopy, recording, scanning, or otherwise - except for brief quotations in critical reviews or articles, without the prior written permission of the publisher.

ISBN: 978-1-80049-403-9

THE 23 IMMUTABLE LAWS OF SELLING

Dedication

This book is dedicated to GOD, the ONE that knew me before I was formed, the Alpha and the Omega, the Beginning and the End, the First and the Last, the Author of the universe!

ACKNOWLEDGEMENT

To God, who gives wisdom and without whom I am nothing.

To my beautiful wife, Maria Riches, whose unwavering support, love and sacrifices made this possible; to my dad, Waleola Moses Awoyinfa, whose repeated words of wisdom echo in my heart always; to my second dad, Mike Awoyinfa, who showed me the value of hard work and dedication; to Barrister Ngozi Ekeoma, for giving me the position and opportunity that allowed me to validate my sales theories; to Musa Jibril for proofreading and editing the manuscript; and to my mentors — Tony Robbins, Brian Tracy, Denis Waitley, Eben Pagan and the rest—I say thank you all from the bottom of my heart.

Table Of Contents

Preface 1

#1: The Law Of Credibility 7

#2: The Law Of Goals 10

#3: The Law Of Identity 17

#4: The Law Of Question 23

#5: The Law Of Competition 27

#6: The Law Of Price 29

#7: The Law Of Number 36

#8: The Law Of Value 39

#9: The Law Of Pain 42

#10: The Law Of Scarcity 45

#11: The Law Of Time 49

#12: The Law Of Entry 51

#13: The Law Of Objection 54

#14: The Law Of Gain 58

#15: The Law Of Desire 62

#16: The Law Of Referral 71

#17: The Law Of 80/20 75

#18: The Law Of Risk 78

#19: The Law Of Upselling And Cross-Selling 81

#20: The Law Of Social Proof (Testimonials) 84

#21: The Law Of Social Selling 87

#22: The Law Of Market Development 92

#23: The Law Of Contrast..97

About The Author 103

Preface

I must give a background on how I came into the sales profession. I had such a poor grade in school that no company would hire me for any other position besides sales. I took it with both hands being the only choice. But I found out it wasn't an easier choice either. I was sacked twice in my first two jobs as a salesman because I couldn't meet my sales quota. Although I used every sales trick and tactic, I knew, but none seem to work.

My whole life was falling apart before my eyes, and I was desperate to fix it. I tried many other things to improve my sales performance; I attended several sales seminars and workshops. I read many sales books hoping they would teach me the secrets of being a better and effective salesman. All of them, unfortunately, failed me.

Whenever I went on a sales pitch, what I'd learnt, the techniques and strategies, never worked. I was still the same old salesperson. Prospective customers still declined to buy my products. Many of them avoided me like the plague when they heard I was around. It was also still difficult to know where to find customers; worse still, it was difficult to know the right words to make them buy. Everywhere I knocked on doors, I heard the same thing over and again: *"Sorry, the contract has been awarded."* Awarded to my competitors, of course. I was beaten black and blue, so to speak, by the competitions.

Some books I read said I should tell the customers more about my products' features and benefits. I did—but my sales results hardly improved. One book taught me fancy sales presentations techniques, which I also used, yet my sales result remained the same. It was a trying time for me. At a point, I began to entertain the dark thought that I probably was destined to fail.

Then I met someone who changed my life.

He can best be described as a sales guru because he was a top performer in his heyday, a much sought-after consultant for Fortune Global 500 companies. A professional salesperson with a wealth of experience, who had amassed stupendous wealth through the profession of selling, honestly, I couldn't have met a better person. Under his guidance, I was transformed into a super salesman.

With hard work and dedication, I learnt and perfected all that he taught me. I even developed a new sales model based on his adopted principles and methods- methods that have worked for some of the world's most successful corporations over the last 99 years. His sales model, painstakingly designed, consists of formulae that will enable even a novice to succeed at selling.

AFTER HIS GUIDANCE AND MENTORING, I went back to the workplace where I was sacked many years ago to work as an independent salesman on straight commission.

Then, the most exciting things began to happen. In three months, I became the highest-selling marketer across the organisation. The company then offered me a paid position as one of its business development team leads. I took the offer and took over the responsibility for the sales performance of 12 other salespeople from that time on. In one month, my team outsold all the other teams in the organisation combined.

Having set the record straight there, I decided to try another industry. Again, I opted for a commission job since I was not ready to take on full employment. In seven weeks, I made the top sales. I was offered a permanent position, but I declined the offer because I felt the industry was not challenging enough. I wanted something tougher, a more significant challenge.

So, I decided to take full employment in an industry I knew little or nothing about and in an organisation locked in cutthroat competition.

It took me a few months to break all their sales records. And I was rewarded with the position of Business Development Executive. In my new designation, I sold millions of the company's products and got them their most valuable clients; for four years in a row, its annual turnover skyrocketed to over 60 million dollars. My billionaire CEO hailed me as the Best Salesman. I became a millionaire to the bargain.

After four years and five months of runaway success, I resigned. The company's CEO gave me thousands of dollars as a parting gift.

SINCE THEN, I have been looking for opportunities to teach others the art and science of sales. I yearned to help struggling businesses discover their sales mojo. It breaks my heart to see salespeople struggling to meet their targets or make a mark in their career. Many people in sales have the drive to succeed; what they lacked is the know-how. Before my turnaround, I, too, had my fair share of disappointment in selling. The frustrations only hardened my resolve to succeed because I had no other option. So, I know how hard the shoe pinches.

Ten years of top performance and extraordinary results validated my sales strategies. The desire to spread the gospel and bring succour to struggling entrepreneurs and salespeople was why I floated Sales Mafia, a sales consulting and training company. We have since helped all our clients to double their sales within the first six months.

"As a general rule," said British Prime Minister Benjamin Disraeli, "the most successful man in life is the man who has the best information." This statement cannot be more accurate for a salesperson—the salesman that succeeds is often not the one with the best product or service, but the one with the best information, the one that acts on the information.

Having and using the right knowledge will save you months and years of pains, heartaches, and disappointments. It will spare you from financial hardship. It will safeguard you from losing the things you worked hard to accumulate.

I am about to share with you sales secrets which are the product of years of hard work, trials, and errors. They are part of the legacies I promised to leave behind. I do not doubt that the information, strategies, and tactics I will share with you in the pages ahead will transform your business, your career and transform your life. Perhaps when you are enjoying the benefits, you might remember to send me a mail to share your success story.

Come to think of it, our life is a continuum of a sales process. In life, we are all salesmen. We are continually trying to sell one thing or the other at every point in our life.

When you were a kid, you tried to persuade your parents to buy you a particular toy; you even tried to convince them to allow you to watch your favourite TV programme when you should be studying for your exams; and when you were older, you tried to sway your employers to give you a job; after a while on the job, you tried to convince them to give you a raise, a promotion. A little older, you tried to sell your lover on how you were the perfect match as a life partner; in marriage, you are always selling your partner what you feel needs to prioritise and what to forgo. All of the processes involved the subtle art of selling.

YOU ARE ALWAYS SELLING, whoever you are. We have all been in this profession longer than we thought we have been. Look at your life and everything happening in it; they result from what you have sold yourself on and what you have allowed other people to sell you on.

With this insight, you have an advantage, not only to become a successful business owner or an employee but also to be an overall success in every aspect of your life. You now have what it takes to get anything that you desire.

Richard Templar, the author of *Rules of Wealth*, regarded the skill of selling as the most essential skill that anyone should acquire. Selling is one of the oldest professions and one of the highest paying too. It has made more millionaires than any other profession in the world. Now that is good news.

Mary Kay Inc. created more women executives, earning an average of $50,000 a year more than any other company in America. It was made possible by educating the women in the profession of selling. A dissection of Fortune 500 companies showed that more senior executives and presidents come from sales and marketing than from any other department in the corporations.

Do you want to become a millionaire too? Good! You can learn and master this skill and use it to turn your life around for good, irrespective of whether you are young or old, educated or uneducated, employed or unemployed, single or married. Whatever you are, you can learn how to sell and use it to make your dreams become a reality. There is no better news than this.

I challenge you today to take this seriously. I challenge you to apply the strategies and techniques in this book to your sales profession—and your business if you have one. I challenge you not to quit at the first time of trying. I challenge you to stick with it until you begin to see results. If there is only one thing that I can guarantee you, it is that these strategies work. They have worked for me. They have worked for many people before me, and they will work for you. It is not a prayer, and it is not a belief; it is a fact!

Sit back and relax as I unveil to you "The 23 Immutable Laws of Selling" that are guaranteed to turn you into a sales superstar.

The 23 IMMUTABLE LAWS OF SELLING

#1

THE LAW OF CREDIBILITY

"Buyers…will not believe the message if they don't believe in the messenger." — James Kouzes, Barry Posner and Deb Calvert

EVERYTHING YOU DO OR FAIL TO DO AFFECTS YOUR CREDIBILITY. In every sales situation, the things you say or don't say, and the way you say them. The questions you ask or don't ask; the advertisements you do and don't do. The way you comport yourself and, yes, the way you dress, all of these will affect your credibility.

A lot of other things also boost or diminish your credibility as a salesman: The length of time you have been in business; the way you conduct your business operations; your level of expertise; your company's financial muscle; the location of your office and the general aesthetics of your business—logo, branding, colours, tone and what have you. Everything that connects to your product, service or organisation can help or hurt your credibility. When it comes to credibility, everything counts. This is why the Law of Credibility is the first law, and invariably, all the other laws help or hurt your credibility.

Does that seem unfair? Unfortunately, this is your reality as a salesman. The world of sales is unfair. It is a world where things can culminate in a deal or aggregate to lose you the deal. To be aware of these things or not, the choice is yours. It is your choice to either play by the rules or to ignore the rules. To be or not to be, it is up to you!

Your goal as a salesperson is to ensure that your prospective customer perceives you in the best light; the higher your score on your potential customer's credibility scale, the easier it will be for you to sell to him. The lower your score, the harder the chance of selling to him.

Credibility is trust in you and your product. Credibility, once established, erases a buyer's apathy, and in turn, stimulates his enthusiasm and arouses the desire to buy.

The possibility of scoring high on credibility with your prospective customers, especially if you are the first point of contact with them, depends on your relationship with them. You must know this: To customers, the best salespeople are F.A.T.—friends, advisers, and teachers.

In Unlimited Sales Success, Brian Tracy writes: "Customers consider best salespeople as friends, advisers, and teachers."

If that is what they think about the best salespeople, then that is what you want to be for them.

To be regarded as a friend, you need to develop a relationship with the prospect; develop a genuine interest in what they do, in the things that matter to them. Have breakfast, lunch or dinner with them. Show them that you want them to do well. Check on them occasionally just to see how they are doing and how the business is doing. Remember: *People like people who like them, and people only buy from people they like.* When you care about their business, they will, in turn, care about your business. When you help them, they will naturally want to help you. It is the law of reciprocity. This form of selling is called "Relationship Selling."

Through "Consultative Selling", you can develop and position yourself as an adviser. As an adviser, you want to sit down with them, take a critical look at their business, and suggest ways to improve. Any suggestion that will help improve or increase their bottom line will always be welcome and appreciated.

In your goal of creating massive credibility with the prospect, you also want to be perceived as a teacher. The only way to do this is to engage in "Educational Selling." Here, your goal is to teach your customer or prospect everything they need to know about your product or services. Because the more they know about your product, the greater their desire to buy—and the greater the possibility that they will help you sell to others through word of mouth.

Your credibility is your reputation. It is your integrity. It is how good you look to the customer. It is to be treasured. Even the Good Book said *a good name is better than riches.*

A good name is hard to forget, and that is what you want. You want to make it difficult for your customers or prospect to forget you so that when they have a business to do, the first person they want to talk to is you. Build up your credibility, and guard it with everything that you have got. It is the lifeblood of your business. It is your most valuable asset.

To build credibility, ask yourself, what can I do for my prospects to show them that I am worthy of doing business with them?

"Without Credibility, you cannot sell anything."

#2

THE LAW OF GOALS

A goal is like a magnet that pulls you towards your desired destination.

HOW DOES GOAL SETTING AFFECT YOUR LIFE?

According to Locke and Lathan (2006), setting goals is linked to self-confidence, motivation, and autonomy.

In 1953, researchers at Yale University sought to understand goal setting's power and conducted a study on graduating students. Their findings showed that 84% of the entire class before graduation had set no goals at all, while 13% of the class had set and written goals but had no concrete plans. Only 3% of the class had both written goals and specific plans.

After 20 years, the 13% of the class that had set and written goals but had not created plans were making twice as much money as the 84% of the class that had no set goals. The researchers were in for further surprises when they discovered that the 3% of the class that had their goals written with a plan had achieved a financial success that was ten times more when compared to the combined wealth of the remaining 97% of the graduates.

A similar study carried out on a Harvard MBA class showed a remarkably similar result. A 2015 study by psychologist Gail Matthews showed that people who wrote down their goals were 33% more successful in achieving them than those who formulated outcomes in their heads.

A sales pro has written sales goals, as well as written plans to achieve those goals. If you don't have a written sales goal, stop reading this now—go, grab a pen and a notepad and write down your sales goals!

There is a power associated with writing down your goals; it is an unseen force that activates and sets in motion a sequence of activities necessary to actualise that goal. Writing down your goals helps you to activate the part of your brain, referred to as the Reticular Activating System (RAS). RAS is the mechanism that brings to your consciousness the things you need to achieve your written goal.

It is like a force that empowers your consciousness to see the resources needed to achieve the written objectives. The moment you write your goal down, you begin to see the things—things that you did not see before—that you need to transform your goal to reality. You begin to see opportunities, people, resources, and methods by which you can achieve your set goals.

Have you ever made up your mind to buy a brand of car or anything, and you immediately start seeing the same car or thing everywhere? That is RAS at work.

At the age of 32, I was earning stipends and still living in my uncle's house. I figured I had nothing to lose by writing down my goal with a specific plan. My goal was to accumulate five million naira (Nigerian currency) in my account within 12 months. With my meagre after-tax salary of N132 000, it would take me 37 months to save this amount, provided I wouldn't spend a dime from my salary. How easy was that? I would have to save everything I earn for the next 37 to 38 months to accumulate 5 million. That's a tall order.

My reality was a far cry: I usually had N6 000 left at the end of the month after all major expenses. At this rate, I would only be able to save N5 million after 500 months! Can you imagine that! Anyway, I wrote my goal on paper, and underneath the goal, I wrote the plans that I thought would help me achieve the goal, then I set to work.

At the end of 12 months, I did not have the exact amount I targeted, but I had N4.5 million in my account. The fact was that I was also a spendthrift at this period because I gave out over N300 000 in cash and gifts to people. I also spent N400 000 above my usual expenses.

To tell you that I was happy to achieve this would be an understatement. It showed me the power that resides in everyone. It showed me that we all have inside us a sleeping giant waiting to be awakened. It showed me the height we can reach if we believe and commit to our goals.

When I saw goal setting's potency, I decided to do it again by setting another financial goal. This time, I set a higher financial goal of N20 million. Again, I did not reach the exact amount, but I was very close. I ended up making N18.6 million within the specified period. During this period, I broke my sales goal and even had my salary increased by my employer. I moved into my apartment and bought a new car. The whole quality of my life increased to the level that I could only dream of.

The secret to setting a practical goal is to use the acronym called SMART.

Specific

Measurable

Achievable

Realistic

Time-bound

Your goal must be specific, concrete, and measurable; you can't improve what you can't measure, and for you to know where you are and where you want to be, you need clarity. Hence, the need for you to set a goal that is specific and concrete. You also must find a way to measure where you are as against where you want to be. What are the things that you can look at that will tell you whether you are making progress or not? What are your key performance indicators? Which metrics are you using to measure your progress?

A realistic goal is an achievable goal; bear that in mind. Sometimes we set unrealistic goals considering our current situation and the deadline we set to achieve the goal.

My advice is to set a goal that you truly desire to achieve. Set a goal that you are passionate about. There is no point in pursuing something whose achievement doesn't excite you because there will be challenges along the way, and it's only your passion for the goal that will carry you through when every other thing fails.

It is also important for you to enjoy the journey, as well. Setting goals is not about achieving the goal itself but also about the person you become. So, the key thing to think about when setting a goal is to ask what will I have to become for me to achieve this goal? Setting a goal that makes you a better person overall should be your goal. Set a goal that stretches you, a goal that forces you to improve your potentials.

Pursuing the financial goal that I set made me more aware of the opportunities around me. It made me a better time manager. It made me cultivate the habit of saving. It made me learn more to improve my skills so that I could earn more. Setting a goal is like creating a **potential activator**. Goal setting activates your potentials!

After the goal has been set, break it down into smaller chunks with a time limit and specific plans attached to individual chunks. Measure your progress on each chunk. If it takes you a longer time to achieve your chunked goals than you expect, then your set time to achieve your primary goal might be unrealistic, and you might need to review it.

Also, you need to continually review your strategy to see if you are moving in the right direction you want to go. If not, you may need to change your plan until you find an effective strategy that moves you in the desired direction and at the right pace.

My final advice on goal setting is this: it is not enough for you to set a goal; you must constantly visualise yourself achieving that goal long before you do. This is perhaps one of the biggest secrets to goal attainment. Ask elite athletes and top performers from various walks of life, and they will tell you the power of visualisation in goal attainment.

Your written goal is the most potent force that pulls you towards creating the life you truly desire. I believe that you cannot live to your full potential until you start setting goals. This is the secret of all self-made millionaires and high performers in every walk of life.

The second part of this law is about your customer or prospect. It is good that you have set your goal as a sales professional, and you are doing all you can to achieve it.

But don't forget that your customer has a goal that he wants to achieve too.

Your success as a sales professional will depend on your ability to know and help your prospective customers achieve their goals.

When a prospect decides to buy your product, he is buying it because he hopes your product or service will help him achieve a particular goal that he has in mind.

Let me ask you what goal do you have in mind when you decide to buy a car? I can guess that you want to move from point A to point B without stress and maybe to show off to your friends and colleagues.

What goal are you trying to achieve when you take coffee in the morning? What goal are you trying to accomplish when you eat, study, marry etc.?

Whatever you do and whatever you buy, you do and buy with a goal in mind.

As a salesman, your job is to find out what goal your prospect or customer is trying to achieve when they decide to buy your product or products like yours.

Why is it important to know the goal that your customer or prospect is trying to achieve when they buy your product?

Consider this illustration: One of the biggest fast-food chains in America wanted to increase its milkshakes sales, and they did everything they knew to make it better so that they could sell more. But despite all their efforts, the sales remained the same.

Then they called in some researchers to help them figure out what else they could do to increase their milkshake sales.

After spending several hours at the fast-food, the first thing the researchers noticed was that half of the milkshakes sold were sold in the morning. As milkshake buyers come and go, one of the researchers decided to ask one of the customers what job are you trying to employ this milkshake to do when you buy it? Initially, the customer seemed confused but upon careful thought and further probing by the researcher, he nodded and said: "I buy this milkshake so that I can have something to engage me and prevent me from sleeping on my long and boring drive to work and also buy some time before having breakfast." Engagement with other customers brought a similar response.

With this realisation, they changed their marketing campaign to match the goal(s) that the customers are trying to achieve when they buy their milkshakes which is "to have something to engage them and keep hunger at bay for some time before having breakfast."

The result: the sales of milkshakes increased four times!

This concept formed the foundation of "Jobs To Be Done Theory" by Harvard Professor Clayton Christensen.

So, go out and ask your customers and prospects what goal are they trying to achieve when they buy your product or service? What job are they trying to get done by buying your product?

Having this insight will unlock your sales potential.

If you don't set goals, you deny yourself of your ideal life!

#3

THE LAW OF IDENTITY

"No knowledge, no sale; absolute knowledge, absolute sale."

MANY SALESPEOPLE EMBARK ON WILD GOOSE CHASES when they search for what is missing in the wrong place. They find themselves hopeless because they do not give enough time to identify their ideal customer.

One evening, I was out shopping when a lady approached me and talked about an offer for a vacation package. She spoke for approximately seven minutes before I asked this question: *Who is the vacation package for?*

"It is for a family," she replied.

To say I was shocked was an understatement.

"I am sorry, but I am still single," I told her, "I do not even have a girlfriend not to talk about getting married."

She looked stupid, sad, and stuttered, "Oh, sorry."

As a good salesperson, her first statement should have been a question to identify if I was an ideal prospect for the vacation package. That would have saved both of us some precious time.

She just assumed that I was married, possibly had kids and had the money to afford her vacation package.

As a rule, never assume the identity of your ideal prospect. Do a proper prospect analysis. The worst thing you can do is to waste your valuable time and resources chasing the wrong person. As a sales professional, managing your time and resources is crucial to achieving your goal.

Amongst other things to look out for when trying to identify your ideal customers are people with the M.A.D. attributes—Money, Authority and Desire. People with **Money**, **Authority**, and **Desire**—they are who you should go looking for.

After identifying a person as a prospect, it will be painful to discover that the person lacks the money, authority, or desire to buy your product or service.

In my encounter with the vacation seller, even if I was married, I certainly did not have the money or desire to go on vacation at that time.

Think about it. You can hardly sell anything to anyone without these three attributes. Having one of these attributes, or two, is not enough; your ideal client must possess all three. It is like a combination code that unlocks a safe. To open the safe box, you must have the exact numbers and know the correct order.

Suppose you have done your homework well in identifying your ideal prospects. In that case, you might discover that majority of your prospective customers may have the Money and the Authority but lack the desire to buy your product or service. That is not bad; it is your job to create in them the desire for your product.

If you have ever read any meaningful sales book or taken any sales course, you would have learnt that at any point in time and in any market, there is always 3% of the market at the top of the sales pyramid that is willing to buy. Hence, if you make a sales pitch to a hundred of your potential customers, you will find three of them ready to buy what you sell at that point. This 3% comprised of the people at the top of your sales pyramid. The second tier, just below the 3% stratum, is occupied by 7% of your market, made up of people in information-gathering mode. These people are open to buying, except that they have not made up their mind about the product or service to choose. Next is 30% of your market: those aware of the problem but not doing anything about it.

At the base of the pyramid is the remaining 60%, which consists of those who are not aware of the problem your product or service solves.

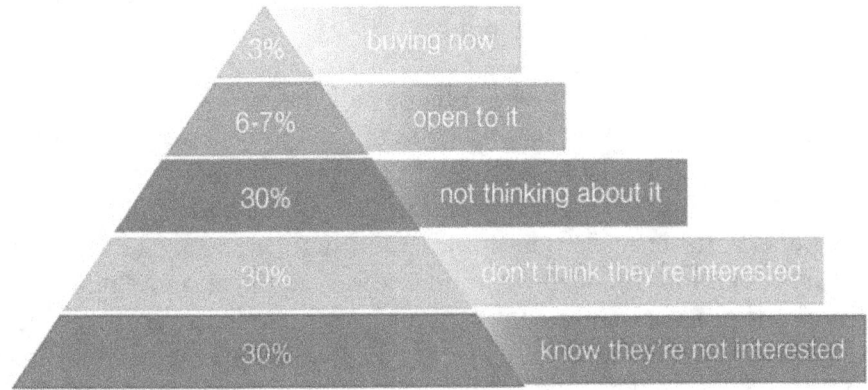

Fig. 1

The level of desire that you must build when you are selling depends on your prospect's position on the pyramid. For a prospect at the bottom of the pyramid, among the 60% who are not aware of the problem, you have a huge task to build and develop the desire to buy. Unlike prospects in the upper part of the pyramid, they know the problems they face and the potential solutions to solve them.

The further down the pyramid your prospects are, the greater the desire that you must build in them to move them to buy.

When you meet your prospective customers one-on-one to make a sale, you want to ascertain that they have these attributes before you go ahead to pitch your sale. When you go to an organisation, the first thing you want to ask your contact person is: *who in this organisation decides concerning stuff like this?* That is the man with the Authority. That is the person you want to be talking to, but before talking to the man with authority, ascertain that the organisation has the money to buy your product or service. When you meet the man with the Authority to buy, get down to your work's final lap, creating the desire to buy your product.

Creating a desire for your product or service might be your biggest challenge as a salesman. But always remember that "how much you know your prospect will determine how much you can create the desire in them to buy your product."

Most of the prospects you will meet as a salesman have unconscious needs. They have needs that they are not even aware of. Your job as a wise salesperson is to probe and push these need(s) from their unconscious into their full awareness. You need to know your prospects' profiles—demographics (sex, age, marital status, health status, education, income, location, etc.). And psychographics (fears, drives, aspirations, motivation, goals, beliefs, likes, dislikes, etc.) and established behaviour patterns, the actual problems they face, and the solutions they are seeking.

However, as I said earlier, the way to know them *in toto* is by understanding them; to understand them is to live in their world. And how do you live in their world? Someone once told me an adage that I found apt: "To catch a monkey, act like a monkey."

The more you know your prospects, the greater your chances of being able to sell to them. *No knowledge, no sale!* It is that simple.

To develop absolute clarity about your customer's identity, every salesperson should create and have what I call a **Buyer Avatomy**— defined as a fictional representation of your ideal customer, built from your research into their demographics and psychographics. It is like an identikit of the perfect customer, complete with features. You can liken it to the human body diagram with all the parts clearly depicted and correctly labelled. Consider your buyer avatomy as an amalgam of the external and internal features of your customer.

Your Buyer Avatomy is a fusion of your customer avatar and customer anatomy.

The **customer's avatar** represents the external features that are easily discernible; this includes gender, age, location, income, marital status, employment status etc. On the other hand, the **customer's anatomy** is the internal features that are hidden and difficult to see and know. It encompasses their pains, motivations, troubles, problems, goals, aspirations, challenges, frustrations, beliefs etc.

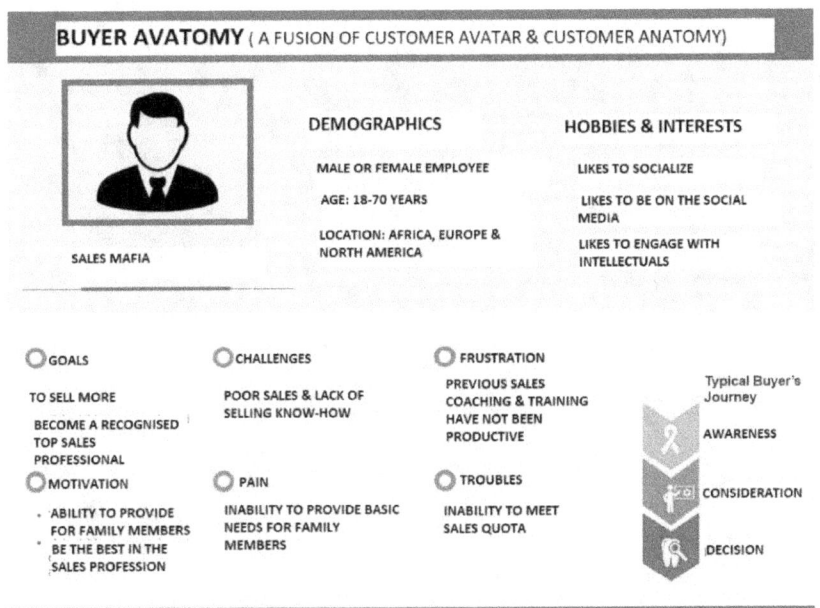

Fig. 2

You should have your buyer avatomy posted somewhere visible in your salesroom or office. It is essential to have it somewhere visible so that you do not have an iota of doubt in your mind as to the kind of person you are looking for every time you are prospecting. This is what creates an absolute knowledge of your ideal customer.

Absolute knowledge of your customer equals an outright sale. No knowledge, no sale.

The more you know about your prospective customers, the better for you as a salesman.

Man, know thy customers!

#4

THE LAW OF QUESTION

The man that has not progressed in life is the one that has not asked the right question!

WHAT HAS THE QUALITY OF LIFE THAT YOU LIVE got to do with the quality of the questions you ask of life?

Over the years, the most powerful and most successful men and women are curious beings who repeatedly asked superior and quality questions.

Take a look at one of the greatest minds that ever lived, Albert Einstein. His most remarkable breakthrough in the field of science came through the questions he asked. These questions drove his Theory of Relativity: Why are initial frames of reference so special? Why is it we do not feel gravity's pull when we are freely falling? Why should absolute velocity be forbidden and absolute acceleration accepted?

There is no gainsaying that the quality of a question determines the quality of the answer.

I can predict your present life's quality if I know the kind of questions you have been asking yourself and others. The man that has not progressed in life is the one that has not asked the right question. Questions control your focus.

Your question is your GPS (Global Positioning System). If you are lost, ask questions!

Questions precede every outstanding achievement and progress in life. The Bible said it succinctly: *Ask, and you shall receive.* That means before you can obtain anything, you need to ask first. This is a great secret that I discovered while I was struggling as a young salesman.

You know every man wants to make money, so the question I asked myself shouldn't surprise you. I asked myself, how can I become a millionaire? I did not stop there; I also apply the Law of Numbers. So, I modified the question thus: *What are the 20 ways to become a millionaire in 12 months?*

This question was the flywheel that turned my life around.

This book is one of the by-products of that question that I asked. That question sent me on a journey of self-discovery and self-mastery. The question created my goals.

Twelve months after I asked this question, I moved out of my uncle's house, where I had lived for 23 years, into my apartment. I bought my car. And still, I had a substantial amount of money left in the bank.

John F. Kennedy, in his famous inaugural address as American President, said, "Ask not what your country can do for you...ask what you can do for your country." This man knew the power of questions; he knew that asking a question is good but asking the right question is better.

When you ask a question, ask with wisdom, ask the right question; if you ask the wrong question, you will get the wrong answer. If you ask a stupid question, you will get a stupid answer. So, don't just ask any question; ask intelligent questions. The better the question you ask, the better the answer you get. *Good question begets good answer.*

Don't ask yourself, why am I such a fool? Or why am I a poor salesman? Instead, ask yourself, what can I do to become a successful salesman? Ask yourself, how can I become a successful entrepreneur in x months or years? How can I be a successful employee in y months or years? How can I be a successful husband and father?

He who asks shall receive, the Good Book said. When you ask, expect to receive answers to the questions that you have asked. When you ask, be ready for the answers. And when you receive your answer, take it, and run with it.

As a salesman, keep a notebook of the likely questions you need to ask your prospects and keep refining them until they begin to give you the perfect answers that you desire.

Like a doctor who asks questions to carry out a proper diagnosis that will enable him to give the correct prescription, you want to ask questions to provide a suitable sales solution. A salesman is also a doctor—a sales doctor in this case. Therefore, you shouldn't jump into giving a prescription without carrying out a proper diagnosis.

Research shows that 87% of customers don't feel that salespeople understand their needs.

It is malpractice for any salesman to suggest his product or service to any customer without first asking questions to ascertain if his product or service is the ideal solution for the customer.

Ask questions about your prospects' challenges, fears, pains, goals, motivation etc. Ask questions to uncover the unconscious needs that your product can help him meet.

Asking questions builds your credibility with the prospect; asking the right questions leads you closer to the sale. Asking questions guarantees that you don't waste your time and that of your prospect. Asking the right questions is one of the most potent weapons in your arsenal as a super salesman.

If you want to get better at selling, you gotta get better at asking questions. —KEENAN, CEO/President, A Sales Guy Inc.

Questions precede breakthroughs!

#5

THE LAW OF COMPETITION

Competition is anything that threatens your market share.

COMPETITION IS ANYONE OR ANYTHING THAT THREATENS YOUR MARKET SHARE. It can be a business entity, an individual or a disruptive technology. Anything at all that can make you lose market share is your competition.

Failure to properly analyse and understand who, where, and what you are competing with can spell doom for you and your business.

To forestall such a bleak fate, you have to ask questions — Who are my competitors? Where are they? What are they doing? How are they doing it? Who are they selling to? Where and when are they selling? What is their market share? What is their strategy? What are they doing right, and what are they doing wrong? How are they different? What is their modus operandi? Why are people buying from them? How much are they selling? — and respond promptly and appropriately where and when necessary.

One of the companies that failed to answer these questions correctly was Kodak. Kodak was in the business of photography. It developed and produced analogue cameras and film and did well at it. Kodak brought photography to people just like Ford brought cars to them. At a point, it had over 90% market share of the global photography business. In 1962, Kodak's sales exceeded $1 billion. But in the 1980s, the photography industry began to shift towards digital photography. Kodak and its management failed to see digital photography as a disruptive technology, so they continued to cling to film-based cameras. They probably hoped that digital photography was a fad that would soon disappear. By the time

Kodak and its management realised that digital photography had come to stay, it was already too late.

On January 19, 2012, Kodak filed for Chapter 11 of the US Bankruptcy Code.

That is the sad story of an organisation that was once a market giant and a trailblazer. The Kodak story is a reality check for everyone and anyone that fails to analyse and understand the competition properly.

You need to study and know your competitors inside out. Because they are your enemies, they can put you out of business and take your market share.

Don't leave knowing them to chance. Buy your competitors' products. Use their services. Visit their worksites and offices. Study how they operate. Observe their follow-up style for prospects and customers. Understand their level of commitment.

What I am saying is simple; it is a three-letter word. SPY on your competitors!

Selling is a game. It is also a war. Don't be caught unaware. Be prepared! Because right now your competition is training!

#6

THE LAW OF PRICE

"The moment you make a mistake in pricing, you're eating into your reputation or your profits." — Katharine Paine, founder, Delahaye Group

ONE THING IS COMMON TO ALL BUYERS. *They want the best deal they can get.* I have not seen anyone that is so rich that he is willing to buy the same thing that others are buying cheaply for a higher price. Whatever you are selling, you just don't want to tell the customer that you have the best product; you want to SHOW them that you have the best deal. And because you are looking at every customer's lifetime value, you can decide to lower your price and make a calculated loss to win customers' trust.

I went to a store for the first time, and I saw a popular product on display at a lesser price than the price tags in other stores. From that day, I became a loyal customer of the store. My thinking is simple: *if they sell this product that I know very well at a lower price, then all their other items are cheaper.*

It took me five years to realise that this store's prices are on the average higher than other stores. The store had deliberately lowered some popular brands' prices to gain customers' trust by creating an impression that "here is a store that gives a better discount on their items." In the process, captivated customers become loyal customers. It is a time-honoured sales strategy.

Henry Ford's business philosophy is, *"Give people the best product at the lowest price."* When other automobile manufacturers raise their prices, Ford lowers his. It is no wonder that he became better known than others. At a time, he was considered the most powerful man in the world.

One store in the United Kingdom put this succinctly in their advert: "If you see an item cheaper elsewhere, within seven days of buying from us, we will refund the difference."

This law has another dimension to it. Because people are poor at determining anything's actual value, they often rely on the product's price or service to determine its worth.

Here is an anecdote about a jewellery shop situated right in the middle of a shopping hub frequented by tourists. For a very long time, the shop displayed a beautiful jewellery piece that no one would buy. The shop owner came in every day to see the gem sitting beautifully on its shelf. She was curious to know why such a jewel was unsold while trinkets were snapped up from the shelves. Why had the salesgirl not been able to sell this piece? The jewellery piece is placed in a vantage position where it was the first item customers stopped to admire once they stepped into the shop. Why it remained unsold wasn't a riddle to the salesgirl. "They lose interest the moment they asked for the price, and I told them its worth," she said.

Sensing that the price was too high, the shop owner instructed the salesgirl to sell the jewellery at "two-times lower the original price " to the next customer interested in it. The salesgirl seemed surprised at this new instruction but decided to obey the owner anyway. The store owner came in the next day to find the piece of jewellery sold. She asked the salesgirl, how did you sell it? "Your strategy was helpful. A tourist who came in asked about the price, and I quoted the new price you told me, and the tourist bought it."

"And how much did I tell you?" The shop owner enquired and was astounded by the price quoted by the salesgirl. The salesgirl had unknowingly sold the piece of jewel at two times the initial amount––and four times the new price approved by the shop owner! How?

The salesgirl had mistakenly processed "two-times lower the original price" as "two-times higher the original price".

With the new price, the piece of jewellery suddenly looked more valuable and worth having for a tourist, no longer a cheap trinket.

David Ogilvy, in his book, *Ogilvy on Advertising*, gave a good example. "In a study of the causes of inflation, the French Government cut thousands of cheeses in half and put them on sale. One half was marked 37 centimes, the other 56 centimes. The higher-priced cheese sold faster. Consumers judge the quality of a product by its price."

The higher you price your product, the more desirable it becomes in the eyes of the consumer.

Yet when Professor Reisz of the University of Iowa tried to relate the prices of 679 brands of food products to their quality, he found that the correlation between quality and price was almost zero.

I am not in any position to tell you what price to put on your product or service. Prices can always be adjusted based on how customers respond to your product. But remember that humans are not very good at placing value on things. Whatever you decide, be fair.

To further help you decide accurately on the right price to charge for your product or service, consider some of these pricing strategies shared by Siegfried Silverman in his article titled "How To Price Your Product and Service":

1. **Penetration Pricing**: This is a marketing strategy used by businesses to attract customers to a new product or service. Penetration pricing is the practice of offering a low price for a new product or service during its initial offering to lure customers away from competitors. Restaurants charge lower pricing at the launch to entice food buyers but later increase the price. I offer my articles for free reading. These articles are later converted into a book for sale.

2. **Price Discrimination**: This is a microeconomics pricing strategy where identical or largely similar goods or services are transacted at different prices by the same provider in different markets. This happens when there is a heterogeneous market; that is, the markets are generally different. You could, for example, prepare a business plan for someone in the USA for, say, US$1000 but charge another person in Africa for the same service only at US$250.

3. **Skimming Pricing:** The organisation sets an initial high price and then slowly lowers the price to make the product available to a wider market. The objective is to skim the profits of the market layer by layer. This pricing strategy was seen in many mobile phone industries where initial SIM cards were sold at higher prices, but prices begin to fall as the year goes by.

4. **Competition Pricing:** Setting a price in comparison with competitors. In reality, a firm has three options: price lower, price the same or price higher than competitors. Some organisations put up a price matching service to check what their rivals are bidding.

5. **Product Line Pricing:** Pricing different products within the same product range at different price points. For example, an instance would be a CD manufacturer offering different CD recorders with different features at different prices—for example, a recordable and non-recordable version. The greater the features and the benefit obtained, the greater the consumer will pay. This sort of price discrimination assists the company in maximising turnover and earnings.

6. **Bundle Pricing**: The organisation bundles a group of products at a reduced price. Common methods are Buy One and Get One Free (BOGOF) promotions. Some organisations are now moving into the regime of Buy Two and Get One Free. This strategy is very popular with supermarkets.

7. **Premium Pricing**: The price is set high to indicate that the product is "exclusive." Examples of products and services using this strategy include Mercedes, Porsche and first-class airline services.

8. **Psychological Pricing**: The seller will consider the psychology of price and price positioning within the marketplace. The seller will charge 99p instead of $1 or $199.99 instead of $200. The method works because buyers will still say they purchased their product under $200, even though it was a dollar away.

9. **Optional Pricing**: The organisation sells optional extras along with the product to maximise its turnover. This strategy is common within the car industry. Vehicles with CD player and automatic transmission sell higher than manual transmission with cassette players.

10. **Cost-plus Pricing**: The product's price is production costs plus a set amount (mark-up) based on how much profit (return) the company wants to make. Although this method ensures the price covers production costs, it does not take consumer demand or competitive pricing into account, which could place the company at a competitive disadvantage.

11. **Cost-based Pricing:** This is similar to cost-plus pricing in that it takes costs into account, but it will consider other factors such as market conditions when setting prices. Cost-based pricing can be useful for organisations or individuals that operate in an industry where prices change regularly but still want to base their price on costs.

12. **Value-Based Pricing:** This pricing strategy considers the product's value to consumers rather than how much it cost to produce it. Value is based on the benefits it provides to the consumer, e.g., convenience, well-being, reputation, or joy. Organisations or individuals that produce technology, medicines, and beauty products are likely to use this pricing strategy.

Now you have all you need to put a price on your product and service. A caveat on price. You would have noticed as a salesman that prospects are always eager to know and hear your price. To an undiscerning salesperson, this looks like a sign of interest from the prospect to buy. You hear something like "how much is it?" or "just tell me the price". Don't fall for it. Most of the time, when a prospect asks for the price before you finish your presentation, it is usually because they are looking for reasons to tune out and walk away from the sales pitch.

A long time ago, my business partner and I went on a scheduled meeting with a multi-million-dollar company's managing director. The managing director had reached out to us to arrange the meeting after he read our proposal. We got to the meeting and started discussing how we intend to help him achieve the proposed goal. And exactly right in the middle of it, he asked, "how much will it cost?" My naïve business partner took this question as a sign of genuine interest and immediately answered with a figure. To cut the story short, the meeting ended there. The MD said, "No". And there was no deal.

Did I know that we had lost the deal when my partner gave a figure in the middle of the presentation? Yes! The moment he opened his mouth and gave an amount, I knew that was the end. Why? Because halfway into the presentation, we were yet to touch on all the things that will drive the desire for our service to the utmost in the prospect's mind; we had not consolidated and hammered on all the pain-points; we had not created a clearer vision of what achieving that goal would mean for his business and his future, and the man dangled a bait, and we took it, hook, line and sinker. And that was the end. *Adios!*

Always remember this: your price should come at the very last part of your presentation. In every sales situation, what you are trying to do is drive up your offering's value to a point where the prospect will perceive your price as a bargain. With your presentation, you want to intensify your prospect's desire and clear all possible objections before you talk about price.

Many skilled salespeople often leave out talking about the price in their presentation, which says two things about you to the customer. First, when you leave out talking about the price in your presentation, the prospect starts seeing you and your organisation as someone that cares more about giving value than receiving a monetary gain. You show that you are more in the business for them than for yourself, and they come first in your business and that making money is not your primary aim. Second, when you don't talk about the price in your presentation, you make it seem as if the price is not important. It communicates to the prospect that you think that your product or service is so good that the prospect will pay for it. That is the law of expectation, which states that people will rise to the level of expectation you have of them. So, if you expect your child to be good, he or she will turn out to be good. If you expect him to do well in school, he will do well in school and vice versa. People always rise to the level of expectation we have of them. You must have once said to someone, "I knew it; I knew you would mess it up." That is the law of expectation playing a trick on you.

So, expect that your prospect will pay the price you charge for your product or service, and you will see it happening more often than not.

Next time a prospect asks for the price before or in the middle of your presentation, simply say, "I will get to that part soon" or "the price is not that important for now, Mr Prospect", or "That is the best part because it is a good deal, and I am sure you will love it."

If you don't expect your price to be an issue for your prospect, your expectation will somehow be communicated to the prospect, and it will make him more receptive to your price without trouble.

Price says a lot more about your brand than just the cost. Price is how you position yourself in the marketplace. Price is the value of the product to the customer.

Remember: Price out of place kills the deal!

#7

THE LAW OF NUMBER

Numbers don't lie!

WE ARE WIRED TO THINK IN NUMBERS. When a number is attached to a product or service, it suddenly makes more sense to us. For example, a body cream that promises to make you look more beautiful on its package without a timeframe as to when to expect the result will not sell as much like the one that makes the same promise with a number on it.

To illustrate this, let us look at two versions of an advert tagline for a hypothetic beauty product called *SoFine*.

Ad Tagline A: "*SoFine*...A beautiful you!"

Ad Tagline B: "*SoFine*...A beautiful you in 4 weeks!"

There is no doubt as to which is better. Tagline B has a stronger stimulus that can trigger prospects to buy than Tagline A.

Tell me, how do you describe someone as rich or wealthy? You most likely say, "He is a millionaire," and better still a multi-millionaire or "He is a billionaire."

Saying someone is rich, and someone is a millionaire, or billionaire triggers different feelings.

You can sell more of your products and services just by injecting numbers into your marketing materials.

Instead of saying, "*Ways to make ladies fall in love with you,*" Why not say "*3 Ways to Make Ladies Fall in Love with You*"? You make it stronger by injecting a number into it.

Which one would you rather buy: *The Immutable Laws of Selling* or *The 23 Immutable Laws of Selling*?

Throughout our lives, we have been programmed to think in numbers. Even the creation of date and time further suggests that we think in numbers. Numbers give us a better picture. Numbers help our mind and brain to understand what is in question.

A number gives clarity; it makes the idea concrete in our mind. Even before you make any purchase, you think of the amount that it will cost you, which is also in number.

Show your customers how long it will take for them to start making a profit from their purchase. As Brian Tracy said, "show them how long it will take for their purchase to become equal to "Free + Profit." If you can show them this, then you can sell anything.

You should also use the law of numbers when telling and showing your prospective customers the value and gain they will get from using your product and service. Don't just tell your prospective customer that your product or service will help them save money. For example, don't say:

Copy A: Our service will help you save money on your production cost.

Rather say:

Copy B: Our service will help you save 30% of your production cost, around $150,000, within 12 months.

You will sound more believable with copy B than copy A. Copy A sounds and looks too abstract and intangible. Your goal is to make your product's perceived value and gain as tangible as possible because your prospect's brain finds it difficult to understand intangible and abstract stuff.

With the law of numbers, you can make intangibles like gains and value more tangible.

The Law of Numbers also affects the volume of your sales. *The more the number of customers you see and the number of calls you make, the more you will sell.*

So, wake up! Call more customers. Go out and meet more customers. Make sure more of your prospects are seeing something from you that reminds them of your product. Get in front of them as often as you can, but don't be a nuisance.

Finally, use market data whenever possible and, if available, to support your claims. As they say, numbers don't lie.

You can win with Numbers!

#8

THE LAW OF VALUE

"To become a success, don't sell a product, don't sell service, sell value."

WHY SHOULD YOUR IDEAL CUSTOMER BUY FROM you rather than from your competitor? The value that your product or service provides is the advantage you have to sell it. The value in your product is your sermon as a salesman. The higher the value on offer than the competition, the higher the price you can charge.

Beyond your product and service value, what other things can you do for your customer as an added value? Are there services or products that you can give out for free that can help your customers? Are there ways that you can help his business grow even if your product is not involved?

Remember that you are in a relationship with your customers for their lifetime value. Like everything, they can get better, too, based on how you deal with them. If you help your customers' businesses to grow, they will, in turn, help your business to grow. It is a law of reciprocity.

Whatever you can do to make your customer better off or make his business run smoothly, do it. You can, for instance, add value to them by sharing a piece of information that can affect their business. When you add value to your customers, they will also be looking for ways to add value to you. It is a principle of human nature. *You scratch my back, and I will scratch yours.*

A customer once came to my office, and as he was about to take his leave, I remembered that I heard some news about a traffic jam that will affect his journey back to his office. I told him and suggested an alternate route. The person has since stopped being a customer; he is now a friend. When a new company employed him, he did not hesitate to give us the company's account to manage, in addition to the account of his former employer that we still retained. That is one of the advantages of treating your customer for their lifetime value rather than as a one-off transaction.

Napoleon Hill summarised it brilliantly when he said, "Instead of saying to the world, show me the colour of your money, I will show you what I can do, reverse the rule and say, let me show you the colour of my service so that I may take a look at the colour of your money if you like my service."

Customers are daily bombarded by thousands of adverts, harangued by an army of salespeople seeking to take a share of their pocket. As the bombardments increase, customers' natural resistance to being sold also grows. They also devised a way of ignoring and overlooking the claims that product owners and services make concerning their brands. Most customers are terrified to buy because their fingers have been burnt many times.

The Three Types of Value

There are three types of value that you can give to your customers, namely: **Financial Value**, **Strategic Value** and **Personal Value**.

Financial value is anything that can help your customer reduce cost or increase revenue.

Strategic value is anything that can help your customers achieve their stated goals or objectives and hence cannot be easily translated into a dollar gain. For example, if your customer's goal or objective is to be more apt in his risk management and your product or service allows him to achieve that goal.

Personal value is the benefits that your customer will enjoy individually if they use your product or service—Peace of mind and a sense of fulfilment are examples of personal value.

Every time you are on a sales call, you must be absolutely clear about the value that your customers will get from using your product or service. And you must find a way to communicate this perceived value to them in a tangible way as much as you can.

Finally, value is anything that you do or give to improve your prospect or business's quality of life. It can be some advice, a discount, or information shared; it can be a listening ear when they need one.

Whatever you sell, always ensure that you maximise your customers' perceived value of your product and service.

The Salesman's Three-Step Value Checklist

Step 1: Ensure that you are clear about your product or service's value for your customers.

Step 2: Ensure that you communicate with absolute clarity the value your product and service will provide for your customer.

Step 3: Maximise your product or service's perceived value for your customers. How? Repeat to your prospect repeatedly during your meeting the value they are expected to get from using your product. Show them testimonials from other customers as proof of the value that they will get.

Use the value they will get from your product to create a vision of a desirable future for them. Better still, find a way to link your product's perceived value to the organisation's ultimate objective.

Doing these will help you maximise your product's perceived value for your customer.

#9

THE LAW OF PAIN

"Speak your customer's language" —**Eben Pagan**

SELL YOUR PRODUCT OR SERVICE BY EMPHASISING THE PAIN that the customers will experience if they don't buy. The usual sales convention is to play up the pleasure customers get if they buy a product.

Now, I say, do it the other way round, whenever possible.

People are more motivated to avoid pain than to seek pleasure. We now know from research that pain not only motivates more than pleasure, but it motivates twice as much.

Dr Nicole Eastman said more starkly: "Pain is my greatest motivator".

Let's interpret the Pleasure-Pain Principle as an equation of Selling where the customer's motivation to buy a product is x—infusing the sales copy with the potential pleasure that the customer will derive from using the product doubles the customer's motivation to $2x$. On the other hand, stating the possible pain that the customer might suffer from not using the product will double his motivation to buy from $2x$ to $4x$.

How does this play out in practice? Let us assume that I sell a patent eye drop called *EG SIGHT* to people above 50. The quality of emotion evoked and its intensity will depend on the copy's underlying principle.

Copy A: "Use *EG Sight* so that you can enjoy your sight until old age." (Pleasure Principle)

Copy B: "Use *EG Sight* to prevent you from going blind anytime soon." (Pain Principle)

Copy B will undoubtedly motivate people to buy more than Copy A because we do more to avoid pain than to gain pleasure!

However, you can better drive home your point with market data or research data. So, instead of using Copy B, you can use Copy C.

Copy C: "Research has shown that men over 50 years of age have a 90% chance of going blind. Using *EG Sight*, a unique eye medicine formulated for men over 50, cuts the percentage to 2%."

Copy C will motivate customers to buy more than A and B because of the market data included. Remember the Law of Numbers?

A pain point is a specific problem that prospective customers of your business are experiencing. In other words, you can think of pain points as problems, plain and simple. **(Source: WordStream)**

Before every sales meeting, ask yourself in advance: *What is my prospective customer's pain point?* The more pain points you can identify, the better. After you have identified these, you want to ask yourself again: *What is the best way to present these pain points?* Your answer to these questions is your sales ticket. It is your sales guarantee.

You cannot become an effective salesperson without using the Law of Pain. Never go into any sales presentation until you have figured out your prospective customer's pain points.

I once used this law even in an interview for a job position. Before the meeting, I'd asked the hiring consultant within the organisation: *what problem are you looking to solve by filling this position?* Once I got my answer, I knew I got the job. All I did was look for several ways to present and represent this pain point and what I will do to help them alleviate it.

Two days after the interview, I got a call from the company's HR, and I was asked to come and pick up my appointment letter.

Fraudsters and blackmailers use pain-points all the time. My job is not to teach you how they use it.

As a salesman, if your prospective customer does not tell you their pain point, it is your job to look for the pain point that your product or service solves and then hammer on it.

Your job is to paint a picture of a pain point that makes resisting your solution impossible. Dig deep.

How far will you go to convince the woman of your dreams to marry you? Your prospective customer is like that woman of your dreams. To woo and win her, you have to bring your A+ game.

10

THE LAW OF SCARCITY

Sometimes, Less Is More!

IS THERE A NEED TO HOARD A PRODUCT THAT IS on the shelf of every shop in town? You often postpone buying a product that you know you need because you know that it is always there whenever you need it.

But you don't do that with a product that you have to seek to find it.

You must create a sense of scarcity for your product.

I once, by chance, experimented with this law. My friend owns quite a big and popular supermarket. And there was a particular product that he stocks in high volume because people buy it a lot.

Then he discovered that the product has not been selling as it used to. This became a concern for him because the stock was tying down a considerable portion of his business capital.

I took a look at the counter and saw almost 100 of the products. I asked him to remove 91 from the counter and keep them in the store, away from customers' sight.

On the counter was left nine of the products. By the next day, at the same time as the previous day that we removed the products from sight, the nine products on display had been sold.

I told him to bring out another nine from the store where we kept the bulk. Before he closed for the day, he had sold the new ones on the counter. He couldn't wait to call me that night to tell me I was a genius.

I had a good laugh because it was no brainer; it is only part of consumer psychology. Now he applies the principle to all the products he holds in large quantity. He just moves them inside and leaves just a few on the counter.

In 1975, researchers Worchel, Lee, and Adewole wanted to know how people would value cookies in two identical glass jars. One jar held ten cookies, while the other contained just two. Which cookies would people value more?

Though the cookies and jars were identical, participants valued the ones in the near-empty jar more highly.

Somehow, scarcity affected their perception of value.

A sense of scarcity increases value. Do you notice how people queue to buy what they will not even use when there is news of impending scarcity? I am sure you see this law everywhere, especially on social media. It is one of the most common selling strategies. You hear common selling lines like "20 copies left" or "two days for the offer to end." Some even put a digital clock so that you can see the number of days and hours left before the offer ends.

It is straightforward: "No Urgency, No Sale!"

A company that understands and uses this law exceptionally well is King.com Limited. King developed Candy Crush Saga, which is perhaps the most financially successful game app in history—raking in almost a million dollars daily.

Candy Crush gives players five lives to use before they have to wait for 30 minutes to continue, and some spots in the game would even require players to wait until the next day before they can continue.

This scarcity strategy creates an unbelievably highly addictive behaviour in the players as they cannot wait to restart the game from where they left off. Even though the game is downloaded free, the scarcity tactics made Candy Crush Saga a valuable game. Activision Blizzard has since acquired King.com limited for US$5.9 billion.

When Noah Kagan created his free email course on marketing, he initially allowed only a seven-day enrolment period. Eventually, he created a waitlist for the second round of enrolments.

Using this scarcity tactic, he tripled his email subscribers, from 12,000 to 50,000, for his OK Dork marketing blog. (Caitlin Johnson, April 26, 2017).

View More on Instagram

648,628 likes
starbucks

As majestic as it is magenta... #UnicornFrappuccino. Color-changing, flavor-changing, potentially life-changing. #🦄 Available for a limited time at participating stores in the US, Canada & Mexico.

view all 37,250 comments

Add a comment...

Fig. 3

Coffee lovers recently raged against Starbucks for adding the "unicorn frappuccino" — made of ice cream, fruit flavours, and sour candy — to its menu. People couldn't get enough of the brightly coloured, highly Instagrammable drink. After stating on its website that the speciality drink would only be **available for a few days**, Starbucks was flooded with unicorn frappuccino orders, and the drink **quickly sold out** on the first day. There are no sales numbers available for the speciality drink yet, but there are nearly 160 000 #unicornfrappuccino posts on Instagram.

Starbucks got many orders — and social media engagement — for another of its notorious **limited-time offer:** the **Starbucks Red Cups**. During the holiday season in December, Starbucks starts serving coffee in red cups for a limited time to drive people into cafes and get them to share #RedCups photos on social media. (Source: HUBSPOT)

The strategy is simple: find a way to create a sense of scarcity for your target audience if you want to sell more!

#11

THE LAW OF TIME

"There is a time for everything, and a season for every activity under the heavens" —**Ecclesiastes 3:1**

HOW DO YOU SELL FISH TO SOMEONE WHO HAD just polished off a sumptuous meal of mackerel? It is disappointing to see salespeople trying to scratch customers when they are not itching. The right thing to do is to scratch when it itches. Don't scratch before it itches. And don't scratch after it itches. Scratch exactly when they are itching.

For a sales professional, timing is everything. Without proper timing, you cannot be a successful salesman. You need to know the exact time when your customers are hungry and serve them.

The idea is to position your message or your product very close to your prospect's time of need. Has anyone tried to sell you snacks after you just had a buffet? Wrong timing!

In Nigeria, I saw a guy trying to sell iced bottled water in the rain. A cup of steaming coffee would have been a better offer. The chance that he will sell many is extremely low. It is a pure waste of effort. Don't try to sell me cold water when all I want is a cup of hot tea.

To be successful as a salesman, you must understand the principle of time and seasons. The timing of your product or service can be the difference between your success and failure. An excellent product at the wrong time will fail woefully. Don't try to sell winter jackets in the summer.

Your understanding of when and where to position your product will increase your chances of success as a salesman.

Many people have prospered, and many have become millionaires just by understanding and obeying the law of time and season. Don't open a breakfast café in the evening.

To understand the law of time is to understand that there is a time for everything. As the Good Book says: "To everything, there is a season and a time for every purpose under the heaven."

You must understand that there is a time to sow the seed of desire for your product or service in the heart of your prospective customer. At this time, you are not going out to sell directly to your customers. You are out to whet their appetite before presenting the main offer.

You will not enter a bar and ask the first lady you meet out on a date. She will probably think you are crazy. You need first to introduce yourself and establish rapport with her. You need to get her to like you. To pull it off, you need to study her and know her likes and dislikes. You need to understand what makes her happy. You need to whet her appetite for you, or else you will not be desirable to her when you offer yourself. Having done all these, you have put yourself in a position to receive a favourable response when you eventually ask her out.

It is the same with your customers, too; you need time to establish a relationship with them. You need time to know them. You need time to get them to like you. The bigger the deal you are proposing, the more time it may take to sow the seed of desire in your prospects. A salesman selling a product or service below ten dollars doesn't need as much time to plant the seed of desire as a salesman selling a product or service that costs hundreds of dollars. The more you know your customers—and the more they like you—the higher your chances of selling to them. It is not rocket science. Many salespeople fail because they want to reap where they did not sow.

Timing is everything!

#12

THE LAW OF ENTRY

"Find customers where they are, not where you expect them to be." —Eben Pagan

KNOW THY CUSTOMER. This goes deeper than identifying who your customers are. It entails knowing where your prospective customers are, where they go, and where you can meet them.

For example, assuming you sell baby care products, like baby lotions and diapers, that means your target is parents with babies, right?

Where do expecting mothers go? They go to hospitals for check-ups, for ante-natal and what have you. For products like baby lotion and diapers, hospitals are one of the customer's access points. A salesman that deals in baby care products, this is where you want to be. This is where you want to position your products. According to the new book written by Robert Cialdini, this is where you want to start your pre-suasion.

This is where you want to start conditioning their minds with a subtle suggestion. You can do this by having your product stands at the maternity ward; you can also do this by giving out free samples of your diapers and lotions to expecting mothers. This is how you start whetting their appetite. Doing this is a sort of advert, putting your product at the forefront of your prospective customers' minds so that when the time comes for them to buy, your product becomes the obvious and the leading choice. You can even make a deal with doctors or nurses for them to recommend your product to nursing mothers. Whatever you can do to make them see your product, do it.

THE BUYER'S JOURNEY AND CONTENT

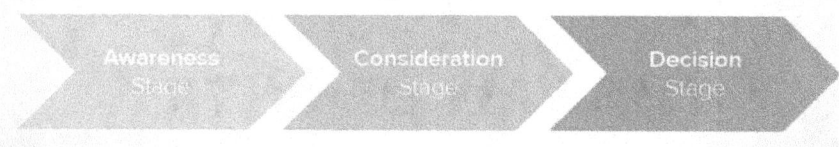

Fig. 4

The process buyers go through to become aware, consider and decide to buy your product or service is known as the buyer's journey.

At the awareness stage, you want your prospective customers to get familiar with their potential need and how to meet them.

Various studies have shown that connecting with your potential customers at the awareness stage in their buyer's journey increases your chance of converting them into a customer than when you meet them at the consideration or decision stage.

The earlier you meet your prospective customers in their buyer's journey, the higher your chance of converting them into a buying customer.

One of your duties as a salesperson is to identify multiple access points to your prospective buyers. When you identify any point of entry, go there, and meet your prospects there. It is such a good strategy that makes selling easier because people are easier to sell when they have not yet decided on the brand they want to buy.

The moment they decide on the brand to buy, it becomes difficult to change their minds. Getting anyone to reverse his choice can be difficult because psychologically, the customer has already identified himself with the product the moment he decides to purchase it.

When a person decides to buy a product or a service, that product or service automatically becomes part of their identity. It becomes part of their definition of themselves. And here is the gain, as Tony Robbins once said: The most potent force in the human personality is the need to remain consistent with how we define ourselves.

Another way of applying this law is to identify the key people in the industry where you operate. I like to call these people influencers. These are people that can influence other people's decisions; some even influence outside of their industries. They are people whose opinions can sway others' buying decisions because they are mostly perceived as experts, while others are admired for their achievement or accomplishment. Just like when you see a dentist telling you the toothpaste or toothbrush to use or a dermatologist that advertises a particular soap for bathing.

It is why so many brands use popular figures to push their products. What you want to do as a sales professional is to befriend these influencers to drive the sale of your product or service.

How can you make these influencers put in kind words about your product or service to their followers?

Note that the relationship must be symbiotic. In the world of selling, there is no such thing as "something for nothing." *It is quid pro quo*—favour for a favour.

Think of how you can also be of value to these influencers. How can you help them achieve some of the goals they want to accomplish too? What are you going to bring to the table?

The vital questions that you want to ask and answer are as follows: ***Who are the people that can help me sell more of my product?***

What do I need to do to gain their confidence and approval?

Where are the possible access points for my prospective customers?

I am asking you to know your customers' touchpoints and use them to your advantage. If you don't, your competitors will.

#13

THE LAW OF OBJECTION

Any objection at all is better than no objection. Objection shows interest.

NOW, ALL YOUR HOMEWORK, HARD WORK and hustling to find prospective customers are finally paying off. You have identified your ideal prospect, and you are face-to-face with him. The only thing between you and making the sale is your prospect's objections.

How do you handle these objections? Brian Tracy in *Unlimited Sales Success* said, no matter what you are selling, customers will have questions and concerns that you must resolve before you can proceed to a sale.

Your ability to handle these questions and concerns is the critical skill that is essential to your sales success. Successful sales have twice as many objections as unsuccessful sales, according to research. Customers who buy raise objections more than those who don't buy at all.

Customers have learnt to say no at first, even to the product or service that they need. Many suffered buyer's remorse after purchases. To stop this suffering, we have learnt to say no to everything. It is an in-built mechanism to prevent us from buying things that we don't need.

A salesperson needs to develop a thick skin for the word "NO". You need to stop taking the word NO personal. Up to 97% of people who will eventually buy from you will first tell you no. So, learn to live with it and be determined that you will never take NO as the final answer.

Some common objections that you can get as a salesman are:

#1: Let me think about it.

#2: Your price is too high; I cannot afford it.

#3: I have a supplier already.

#4: It is not in our budget for this year.

#5: I need to discuss it with my partner.

#6: I will give you a call when I am ready.

According to research, any salesperson will get an average of six objections. Your job as a sales professional is to know all the possible objections that your prospective buyers can come up with and answer them in advance before you go out to sell.

Most of the time, the only barrier between you and that sale is the objection; your ability to answer this objection will be the difference between your success and your failure.

A few ways to handle objections are:

- *Have testimonials from your previous customers that answer some of the objections.*

For example, one of my prospective clients once said that my sales training price was too high. And I said: "You are very right. Some of my best clients say that too at first, but after using my programme and seeing the result, they confessed that it is the best decision they ever made as regards sales training."

I then went ahead to show him a testimonial from one of my clients that says, "I thought the price was too high, but after a year of increased sales and more customers, I realized that the training has more than paid for itself and even left me with a big profit going with it. Thank you for talking me into this."

The trick is to agree with the prospect on whatever objection he raises, then move swiftly to answer the objection.

- *Use a comparison chart to show the performance of your product in comparison with your competitors.* You can show him a publication about your product. Whatever you have to do to answer the objection, do it.

- *Try to be agreeable while working around the objection.*

When your prospects make objections, you don't want to disagree with them outrightly; if you do, you will make them feel stupid for raising that type of objection, and that would defeat your aim.

Assuming the prospect says: let me think it over.

You may want to say: "That is good, Mr Prospect, because it is a crucial decision to make, and I am sure you have a reason to want to think it over. May I ask what the reason is?"

Your goal is to make them like you by being agreeable with them. Then you systematically answer their objection using all the weapons in your arsenal. You can even make a call to one of your loyal customers on the spot in other to answer the objection. Sometimes, the objections you will hear can sound and feel very stupid but do not get angry because any objection at all is better than no objection. Objection shows interest.

- *Confirm the real objection!*

You want to be sure that you are answering the real objection. Anytime there is an objection, dig deeper to be sure that it is the only and the real objection so that you don't waste your time trying to answer someone that just wants you to go.

When, for instance, a prospect says, "It is not in our budget,"

You may respond this way: "Mr Prospect, that is understandable, but assuming it is in your budget, will you take it now?"

If he says "yes," then move in with this line: "When is the next budget, and can we have an agreement in place before the next budget?"

If the budget is not the real reason, the prospect will bail out at this point. And that will signal that it is not the real objection. In that case, you continue to dig deeper to get the real objection out. You can say: "Clearly, that is not the only thing on your mind Mr Prospect. May I know the other concern you might have regarding this product?"

Be pleasant, and do not be in a hurry to answer the objections. Remember, no objection, no sale.

#14

THE LAW OF GAIN

What's In It For Me (WIIFM)? WIIFM is everyone's favourite station!

THE ART OF SELLING CAN BE TRICKY SOMETIMES. Most times, the people that buy from you are not the end-users, but somehow, they are the ones that get to decide whether to buy your product or not.

It often happens with products that are commodities, and it happens with standard services, especially those that do not require much expertise. For example, if your car is dirty and needs refuelling, you may ask your driver to fill the car at the gas station and take the vehicle for cleaning. He alone decides where he wants to go. The same applies to the purchase of office stationery which the secretary or receptionist can do. Or the selection of a supplier of building materials for an organization's building project can be determined by the human resource manager who knows little or nothing about what to look for in a good construction company and who, himself, is not the end-user.

So, how do you position your product or service to be uppermost in the minds of these people? What can you do to become the chosen one?

You need to understand that everyone, virtually everybody, does something for something. Here we go again: *Quid pro quo*. No one does something for nothing. Most business owners are in business for profit; others are in it for the joy, happiness, and satisfaction that it gives them. Ultimately, everyone is doing something to meet a need, so it is safe to say that we are all doing the things we do for the gain. It could be personal gratification or monetary gain.

Therefore, it is necessary to identify the need, in this case, "The Gain" that you are helping your clients and affiliates meet, whether directly or indirectly.

Be that as it may, everyone's favourite station is the WIIFM— *What's In It For Me?* I can guarantee you that if you can answer the WIIFM question for your clients and affiliates, you have a business that can truly thrive in any environment. The need that you help them meet becomes their motivating factor to come back to you.

Every time you are talking to a new prospect, the prospect is screaming in his head, *what's in it for me?* He is saying in his subconscious: *cut all the crap and show me what is in it for me, then I will decide if it is what I want or not.*

Even when you are talking to facilitators or third parties, all they want to hear is the WIIFM station.

Now ponder these couple of questions: Is it possible to meet people that are not the end-users of your product or service but can connect you to the end-users of your product?"

Of course, yes!

Will these people be more open to helping you if you show them what is in it for them?

That means you can maximize your profit from all your meetings. You don't always have to meet the end-users. But for everyone you meet in the chain that leads to your sales, there must be something for them. This is the secret to breaking boundaries because most of these people will do things you cannot do to ensure that you get to the primary decision-maker or the man with the money and authority.

They will cross the ocean for you to make the deal happen because of what they also stand to gain. The WIIFM station is the only station that everyone tunes to. It is a universal station that speaks the language that everybody understands.

So, learn to speak the language – the favour-for-favour language– speak it with precision and see yourself selling more than you can handle. It is a salient truth about the world of selling, a world where nothing goes for nothing—the world of *quid pro quo*.

Some years back, I had two friends. One was the Human Resource Manager from the company I resigned from. The other was a casual friend who worked with another organization specialising in training organizations' workforce to improve performance.

My friend in the management training firm wanted to sell some training courses to my company through my friend, the Human Resources manager. But the HR manager wouldn't accept or even consider his proposal. The former told me about his challenge and asked me to help him put in some kind words, so the latter would give him a chance.

I told him: "No. That is not how to sell your services. I can help you put in some kind words here, but it will only get you this business. How do you intend to get another business if this happens in another organization where you don't have anyone to put in kind words for you?"

He was blank for a while. And I said to him, "I won't put in any word for you, but rather I will teach you what you need to do to make your sale."

Step 1: Go back to the HR manager and find out his goal, desire, and dream regarding his present job and career.

Step 2: When you find out his career goal, propose to him one of your training programs to help him move closer to achieving his career goal, desire and dream. And train him for free! This will answer the WIIFM question for the HR manager.

Step 3: After he has completed the training, go back to him concerning your initial proposal, which is to train other organisation staff.

Two weeks after our discussion, my friend came back elated. My HR friend had finally considered and submitted the proposal, and Management approved some of the training courses for 50 members.

By answering the WIIFM question for your prospect, you will be fulfilling two fundamental selling laws, namely, the Law of Gain and the Law of Goals.

#15

THE LAW OF DESIRE

Desire is the weapon of your warfare against the competition!

EVER SEEN ANYONE BUYING SOMETHING THEY LOATHED? Like you are inside a store, and this dude walks in and says: "I want to buy this product because I hate it!"

Did I hear you say it can't possibly happen? You are correct because what precedes every buying decision is desire, not loathing.

A salesman's job is to create that desire before the sale. The greater the desire you create for your product, the easier it is for you to sell. So, a sales professional is always thinking, *how do I create the desire for my product?*

It is like seeing a lady you wish to date; to make headway, you have to make her desire you.

How do men invoke desire in a female love interest? Some men do this by bragging—telling her about all their achievements, their status in the society, the amount of money stashed away in their bank account; some men resort to showboating. They flaunt their flashy cars—some show-off their biceps and six-packs—anything it takes to generate the desire in her.

If you cannot get her to desire you, then your chance of getting her to date you become very slim. Similarly, a sales professional thinks and looks for ways to use what he has and knows to create this desire in prospective clients.

Desire equals sale; lack of desire equals no sale. When you are hungry, your desire for food increases; food, in this case, becomes the only thing that can stop hunger. It is up to you to decide the type of food you eat.

How will you position your product to become the food your clients choose to eat when they are hungry? What will you do to make your food more palatable and attractive? How will you prepare it? How will you serve it? How will you convince them to have a taste?

How do you create a craving that only your product can satisfy? The key to creating the right desire is knowledge. Knowledge about the needs and wants of your prospects. Knowledge of how to create and trigger your products' desire in the mind of your prospective customers.

The Psychology of Creating Desire

Understand this today, the weapon of your warfare against your competition is not external but **Internal**; and this internal weapon is strong enough to break down every resistance of your prospects! This is a secret that many salespeople, marketers and entrepreneurs don't know. They think that creating a great product will translate into sales success, while some believe that slashing and lowering their prices will guarantee unlimited sales. These things cannot be further from the truth. We have seen that the lowest prices do not always guarantee sales success and that higher quality does not always translate into higher market share.

What creates torrential rain of sales for your product and service is not the lower prices you fix or the higher quality you delivered; instead, it is the Desire level you create for your product and service. Salespeople, marketers and entrepreneurs that rely on the lowest prices and highest qualities made the fundamental mistake of thinking that we are "logical beings with emotions" when in reality, we are "emotional beings with logic." *We first make our decisions emotionally; then, we try to justify those decisions logically.* One of the most respected psychologists alive, Daniel Kahneman, said the primal brain (which can also be called the emotional brain) still rules today. We, *Homo Sapiens*, are 99% at the mercy of our primal brain. So, it is easy to say that we are 99% at the mercy of our emotions.

Antonio Damasio, a US neuroscientist, said, "We are not thinking machines that feel. We are feeling machines that think."

So, the question that comes to mind now is what is Desire?

The Oxford dictionary defined Desire as a **strong feeling** of wanting to have something. The same dictionary described Emotion as a **strong feeling** deriving from one's circumstances, mood, or relationships with others.

It is, therefore, safe to say that Desire is an Emotion.

So, it is not an assertion when I say again that what controls your prospects' decisions about whether to buy or not to buy your product is not logic but **emotion**. Emotion is energy in motion, and this energy is the source of all our decisions. Emotion is to our brain what fuel is to an engine. Without fuel, the engine is useless and can do nothing.

In *Psychology Today*, Michael Levine affirms that emotions drive 80% of Americans' choices and that rationality only represents 20% of human decision-making.

With this insight, I want to reveal the six ways to create your product's desire in prospective customers' minds.

Six Ways to Activate Desire

1. Make it about them (Customer-centric)

2. Make it easy to understand

3. Use visuals all the time

4. Make your products benefits-tangible

5. Make it memorable

6. Create contrast

Please don't take this list with a pinch of salt because it results from exhaustive research in neuroscience and neuromarketing. Each item on the list creates a massive opportunity for you to activate and boost the level of desire for your products and services in your target audience's mind.

Remember, the greater the desire, the lower the resistance. According to Harvard Professor Gerald Zaltman, 95% of our purchase decisions are made unconsciously.

Make it about your prospects

For your product and message to be accepted by your prospects, you must find a way to make it about them. Your product and marketing messages must be prospect and customer-focused. Your company's story and why you do what you do must be centred on your prospects and customers. When your story centres on them and focuses on them, you help them establish an emotional connection with your product, brand, and company. Make your customers the central characters. Make them the actors in your movies, and you will be able to take them on an emotional ride that will sway their decisions to buy from you (More on this under the law of contrast).

Make it easy to understand

Research shows that humans tune out messages that are hard to decode. Hence, the key to creating marketing messages or sales messages that will hit a home run with your audience is by making it very simple. The harder it is for your message to be understood, the harder it will be for you to sell. Can you imagine how difficult it will be to sell to someone who doesn't speak your language?

In psychology, we refer to the ease with which we process information to understand what that information means as **Cognitive**

Fluency. Hence, studies have shown that the higher the cognitive fluency, the higher the conversion rates. Put another way, the easier it is for people to understand your message, the easier it will be for them to buy from you.

In an article titled "How Cognitive Fluency Affects Users Behaviour", Jon Barber described an experiment in which two psychologists Hyunjin Song and Norbert Schwarz, presented a paper that described a workout routine and a recipe for preparing sushi. The texts were written in a font that was easy to read and a font difficult to read. Students who received the text in the easy-to-read font believed that the instructions were easier to follow than those who received the text in the complicated font.

So, even in your product design as an entrepreneur, you must always think about the ease of use for customers. People don't like anything too complicated because it takes more energy to process. The more energy that I need to do something, the less likely I am to do it. That is why so many people skip going to the gym even when they know they must maintain good health. It is the same reason why so many students run away from mathematics because they feel it requires more energy to comprehend.

Research findings indicate that for your marketing or sales message to be highly effective, it must be understood by a 4-year-old. Why? Because a 4-year-old has only the primal brain, if a 4-year-old cannot understand your message, then you should consider making it simpler.

Use visuals all the time

Out of the 100 billion neurons in our brains, 30 billion are visual neurons. The result is that we respond better to visual stimulus than other sensory inputs. Do you remember the popular saying that a picture is worth a thousand words? It takes an average of 14 milliseconds to process an image, while it takes 140 milliseconds to process a word.

If you want to persuade people, you need to use more visuals!

Make your products benefits tangible!

To effectively persuade your prospects to buy, you must make your product benefits, values and gains projected as tangible as possible. It is because the human brain struggles to understand intangibles. When something is tangible, it is simplified. Under the Law of Value, don't tell the customer that your product will help them save money on their production cost; anyone can make that claim. After all, a dollar saved is still money saved, right? Tell the customer the number of dollars that your product has saved other customers in production cost. "Customer Y was able to save $50,000 in production cost in a year, and from our rough estimation, this product can also save you $75,000 in a year and $750,000 in ten years."

Remember, Tangible is Simple and Understandable!

Make it memorable!

Whether it is your message or product, make it easy for the prospects to remember. You want your prospects to remember your product and message at the point of decision of whether to buy from you or your competitor. Therefore, you must follow all the previous steps that we have discussed. Finally, whatever your value propositions are, don't let them be more than three at a time. Why? Because the brain finds it difficult to remember items that are more than three at first. Also, use the power of repetition. For example, Sales Mafia value propositions are:

- ❖ Sell More

- ❖ Sell Faster

❖ Sell Now

Another company, called CodeBlue, also uses three claims too:

➤ Extraordinary Speed

➤ Extraordinary Science

➤ Extraordinary Service

After adopting the three claims, CEO Paul Gross reported a 34.87% revenue increase in nine months, representing a 50% increase in annual growth.

And yet another company, Innovative Office Solutions, also uses three claims:

o Expect Response

o Expect Reduction

o Expect Relief

The CEO Jennifer Smith has this to say: "Seven years ago we started to use a clear set of three reasons why our customers should buy from us (our claims). As a result, our business today is seven times bigger than seven years ago, hitting $100M in revenue."

The problem with most of us is that we want to be everything to everybody. So, we want to make all the claims, and, in the process, we lose the most important people to us; our target audience.

The best scenario is to be remembered for just one thing, like Volvo, which is widely remembered for Safety and Mercedes that is synonymous with Luxury, which means that you *ought to* have only one claim. But I understand that this might be a tall order in this current business clime. Hence, it is okay to have three—but not more than three claims. Anything more than three is unacceptable.

Another way to make it memorable is to rewrite your claims into a rhyme. Why? It will help you trigger the rhyme-as-reason effect, which Wikipedia defined as a cognitive bias whereupon a saying is judged as more truthful when it is rewritten to rhyme, illustrated with these two brilliant examples:

Statement 1: What sobriety conceals; alcohol unmasks.

Statement 2: What sobriety conceals, alcohol reveals.

Statement 2 was adjudged more truthful than Statement 1, even though both are the same.

The Rhyme-as-reason effect is one of the 188 cognitive biases that influence our decisions.

The famous American lawyer and civil activist Johnnie Lee Cochran Jr. knew the power of cognitive bias when he coined the famous rhyme line **"if it doesn't fit, you must acquit!"** in defence of O.J. Simpson for the murder of his ex-wife and her friend. The magic line, repeated throughout the trial, got his client eventually acquitted.

Patrick Renvoise, Co-founder and President of SalesBrain, gave another great example in his book *The Persuasion Code* of a company called CDF for Labour Law, a successful law firm specializing in California Employment Law. Their three claims are: Protect your time, Protect your dime and Protect your peace of mind.

First, notice the repetition of the word **protect**, which creates a rhythm; then the use of the word **your**, which triggers your customer's primal brain because it is customer-centric, and finally, the rhyme of **time, dime, mind.**

What are your three claims, and how can you make them rhyme?

Read the Law of Contrast to see how to use the last element, *Contrast,* to persuade your prospective customers.

#16

THE LAW OF REFERRAL

"Referral business closes and converts 70% of the time."

If you have satisfied clients referring more people to your business, then you might never need to cold call again in your life.

That has always been my lot in all my sales jobs. I discovered that the hard part of selling is usually in the early days when I had not built my client base—earlier days when I used 80% of my time prospecting. I checked Facebook, LinkedIn, Twitter, Google, websites, yellow pages etc., to gather information about my prospective clients.

The moment I got up to ten customers, my cold calling stopped. I started asking each of my clients for six referrals at the very least. And I had a 70% closing rate on the referrals, who gave me more referrals to call on. Perhaps your most effective weapon for ensuring that your sales pipeline is consistently filled as a sales professional. And if you are not using it, that means you are wasting your effort, time, and money. I even tell my loyal clients to help me call some referrals in advance to inform them that I will call later.

Make it personal.
84% of B2B buyers start
their buying search with a referral.

Source: SuperOffice

Fig. 5

When I finally meet these referrals, I usually start with, "Oh, Mr Prospect must like you so much to introduce you to me; how did you guys meet, by the way?" This question is always an icebreaker because it gets them to come out of their shell. They all usually start with a smile on their faces as they recall how they met. And it allows me to have an angle on them and know them better. As we have already started the relationship on a good note, they feel like I already belong in their circle, and hence they see me as a friend. And remember, people buy from people they like; therefore, selling to a referral is way more comfortable 90% of the time.

Erin Woods, a research and strategy author, suggested that you can even have a referral programme in an article. According to her, implementing a referral programme encourages your brand's existing customers to become brand advocates and promote positive brand awareness among potential customers. She suggested six different referral programmes, but the two I found most interesting are Referral Contests and Scaled Referrals.

Referral Contests: Woods theorizes that innate competitiveness lies within many people. You can bring this out in your existing customers and expand your client base simultaneously with a referral contest. To ensure success, you'll need to establish a sense of urgency among participants. The contest should be set for a specific duration of time when referrals can be submitted and when the referral must sign up. Whichever customer submits the most referrals (that decide to sign up for your company's services) within the time frame wins a prize. Customers are more likely to participate if they believe they have a good chance of winning. So, you may want to entice people further to partake by offering prizes for second and third place winners. One of the primary keys to a successful referral contest is ensuring your customers are aware of the contest in the first place. Focus your promotion efforts on generating a buzz around the great prizes your firm offers to the winners because this is what customers are interested in. The prizes offered should be more enticing than a standard referral programme since there are fewer winners, but still within your budget.

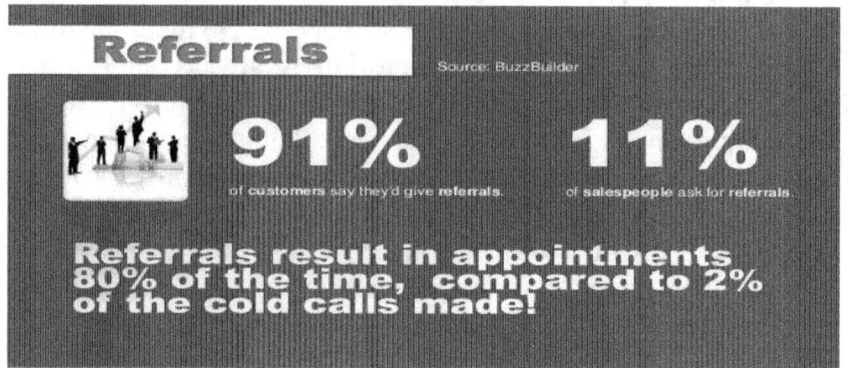

Fig. 6

Scaled Referrals: With scaled referrals, there are not just one or two winners. A scaled referral programme rewards everyone and uses the simple idea that the more referrals customers bring in, the higher their rewards. For instance, the first referral a customer brings in will receive a $50 reward, for the second referral $100, $150 for the third referral, and so on. We recommend setting a cap for the number of referrals a customer can bring while receiving the bonus rewards. After the cap, they would receive the standard referral reward your firm offers.

Personally, the scaled referral is my favourite, and I will encourage every salesperson out there to take asking for referrals more seriously. Find a way to reward your customers for any help they render to you or your company. The reward doesn't always have to be monetary. Experiment with other things that you can do for your customers that they can appreciate. It can be free consultation or whatever you think will be valuable to them. But take your time to find out if they value your reward. Nobody wants to do something for a reward that is not valuable to them.

With your referral programmes, you will also be cementing and building a stronger long-term relationship with your customers.

Sell more with referrals!

#17

THE LAW OF 80/20

Selling is 80% listening and 20% talking!

EVER HEARD OF THE 80/20 RULE? Yes, of course, the world-famous Pareto Principle! The principle was suggested by a management consultant, Joseph M. Juran, named after an Italian economist Vilfredo Pareto who observed the 80/20 connection while at the University of Lausanne in 1896 published in his first work *Cours d'Économie Politique.*

Pareto showed that 80% of the land in Italy was owned by 20% of the population. Pareto argues that 80 % of our result comes from 20 % of our effort. That means 80 % of all your sales come from 20% of your clients.

Perhaps, you didn't know; from today, be aware that not all your clients are equal. Some clients have more value than others. That means you cannot afford to devote EQUAL time and effort to all your clients.

Let me paraphrase: *Some customers are more valuable than others.*

Just as you start prospecting, you will notice that some prospects are excellent while some are bad prospects. When you see lousy prospects, don't waste your time on them—MOVE ON.

Bad prospects are the ones that never get to make up their minds, whether to buy or not. They are the ones that will ask you to keep calling back. They are the ones that will want to price you out of your profit. They are the ones that make unnecessary and unrealistic demands. Once you realised who they are, please don't waste your effort on them. Let them go.

When I was a business development executive in an oil and gas company, we were referred to a company with over 1000 buses deployed for mass transportation. We were in this organization for weeks trying to get them to do business with us.

Finally, we got the account and the first order they placed was for the supply of two million litres of Automotive Gas Oil. Phew! In the first year of our business relationship, we supplied over ten million litres of automotive gas oil for their buses, which was more than the total we had done in six months in the company's entire retail business. Those outside my department used to wonder why we visit them almost every week. Now they know why.

So, here are some Pareto 80/20 rule examples:

- *In customer service, 80% of the complaints come from 20% of your customers. (HUBSPOT)*

- *20% of a company's products represent 80% of sales. (HEFLO)*

- *20% of employees are responsible for 80% of the results. (HEFLO)*

- *20% of a company's salespeople make 80% of the sales.*

- *80% of your company's revenue is generated by 20% of your customers.*

Your job as a crack salesperson is to identify that valuable 20% of your clients that bring 80% of your profit and protect them with all you have. They are like golden eggs that must not be broken.

I am not saying that you should not look after other customers, too. Set your priorities right; that is what I am saying. What you want is more of this 20% in your bucket. They are the ones that will keep you in business.

The second part of this law is what I consider to be the most important because this is where most salespeople get it completely wrong! Often, when salespeople meet prospective customers, they think it is an opportunity to dive into rhetorical appeals about how good their products and services are and why they should be selected.

Instead, you are supposed to use this time to listen more and talk less. Many salespeople had talked past the sales and left the customer more confused than before they met. Countless research shows that the most effective salespeople listen more and talk less.

When you listen to your prospects, don't just listen, but listen actively. Listen to find a way to help them solve their problem. Listen and talk like the sales doctor that you are.

When you begin to listen more than you talk in every sales situation, then you set yourself up to truly become the best that you are capable of becoming.

#18

THE LAW OF RISK

"Customers will choose lower-risk products and services at higher prices over higher-risk products and services at lower prices."

WILL THIS PRODUCT DO WHAT IT SAYS IT WILL DO?

The extent and clarity with which you can answer this question while selling will determine your chance of closing a sale.

Customers will always choose lower-risk products at higher prices over higher-risk products at lower prices.

You might need to read that again to understand and fully grasp it.

One of the duties of a good salesperson is to reverse risk for his clients. A sales professional takes the risk on behalf of his clients. Some call it "risk reversal." Some call it a "guarantee." The more you can lower the risk associated with buying your product, the higher your chance of making the sale.

Most people run away from buying even the things they need and want because of the risk involved. The higher the product's price in question, the higher the customer's worry about the risk involved.

How do you guarantee your prospective clients that your product will do what it says it will do? How do you alleviate the fears of unknown pain for your potential customers?

You can do this by letting your prospective client try out the product before committing to it.

Claude Hopkins narrates the anecdotes of two horse sellers and an electric machine seller to illustrate this point in his book, *Scientific Advertising*.

"Two men came to me, each offering me a horse. Both made equal claims. They were good horses, kind and gentle. A child could ride them.

"One man said, "Try the horse for a week. If my claims are not true, come back for your money." The other man also said, "Try the horse for a week." But he added, "Come and pay me if my claims are true." I naturally bought the second man's horse."

"The maker of the electric sewing machine motor found advertising difficult. So, on good advice, he ceased soliciting a purchase. He offered to send to any home, through any dealer, a motor for one week's use. With it would come a man to show how to operate it. "Let us help you for a week without cost or obligation," said the ad. Such an offer was resistless, and about nine in ten of the trials led to sales."

Nordstrom, one of America's most successful department chains, understands the power of this law more than many: it offers a lifetime guarantee on any product that you buy from any of its stores.

If you can reduce the risk to the barest minimum or remove it entirely for your customers, you will experience a surge in sales. This alone can double your sales because it automatically increases your credibility. People will begin to trust you and your product more. It makes you and your product look more attractive.

As a sales professional, what are you ready to risk? What are you willing to risk for the buyer for him to know that you are genuine and that you can be trusted? You cannot expect the buyer to take all the risk by dropping their hard-earned money for a product they are not familiar with.

What can you put on the line for your prospective buyer to feel more comfortable doing business with you? Can you deliver the result that you promised before collecting your compensation?

Car wash services do this well. They wash your car first before asking for payment—value before the reward.

Is there a way you can do something similar? A mattress company in the UK understands this law so well that it changed its sales model by sending the mattress to prospective customers to use for 200 days before asking them to pay or return it. They even deliver the mattress to your home and pick it back after 200 days if you are not interested. All at no cost to the prospect!

The world of selling is more brutal than it has ever been. Either you play by the rules, or you will be left in the dust.

#19

THE LAW OF UPSELLING AND CROSS-SELLING

You're 60-70% likely to sell to an existing customer, compared to the 5-20% likelihood of selling to a new prospect. —Sophia Bernazzani

ACCORDING TO RESEARCH, IT COSTS SIX TIMES more to get a new client than it does to sell something to an existing client.

When I newly arrived in the UK, I needed a personal computer. I walked into a popular electronics store and looked around to pick my choice. Just before I made the payment for the laptop, the salesman said, "Would you like to purchase our installation package?" I ended up purchasing an installation package that is almost half the PC price that I bought. It is a classic example of cross-selling.

Cross-selling is a strategy to sell products related to the one a customer already owns or is buying. It is like going out to buy a bed frame, and the seller tries to sell you a mattress with it. I had gone into the store to get a personal computer only, but I ended up buying the PC and the installation package.

On the other hand, upselling is a strategy to sell a superior, more expensive version of a product that a customer already owns or is buying. Car manufacturers and retailers do this regularly. They call their existing customers to offer a newer model or version of the car they already own. And so many people go for it.

Organizations that excel in sales find a way to upsell and cross-sell to their customers. Likewise, a sales professional that excels in sales finds ways to upsell and cross-sell to customers.

Up-sell   &   Cross-sell

Fig. 7

You don't have to be the manufacturer or producer of what you upsell or cross-sell. You can upsell and cross-sell through affiliation.

It is a surprise that most business owners and salespeople don't take this massive opportunity to sell more and bond more with their customers. Because the more a customer buys from you, the more they feel attached and thus bonded to you. The more they buy from you, the more they trust you.

Upselling and cross-selling are way easier than you think because you already have the customer's trust to an extent, at least enough to make the first purchase. So upselling and cross-selling them wouldn't be as difficult as making the first sale.

It is not surprising that Candy Crush Saga is considered one of the most successful game apps in history. Activision Blizzard, the game app owner, uses a combination of laws of selling to their advantage.

Apart from using the Law of Scarcity, as shown earlier, they also use the Law of Upselling and Cross-selling beautifully. The game is designed with multiple levels, and the success and progress of individual players in the game means climbing the success ladder, designed as different levels in the game. Climbing this success ladder, however, comes at a price. Users pay a certain amount to be able to move to the next level.

Candy Crush Saga is continually creating and launching new and higher game levels to entice players to keep playing and keep paying. On average, a new level is released every two weeks.

For me, this is an upselling and cross-selling masterstroke.

So, if your company isn't cross-selling and upselling, you're just leaving money on the table. —Sophia Benazzani

#20

THE LAW OF SOCIAL PROOF (TESTIMONIALS)

Customers' testimonials have the highest effectiveness rating for content marketing at 89%—Social Fresh

HAVE YOU EVER BOUGHT SOMETHING BECAUSE someone else bought it, or because someone said something good about it, or because someone recommended it directly?

When I am in a new neighbourhood, I usually look out for restaurants where several people are eating. Seeing several people is a sign that the food is good. Sometimes I try to check the restaurant's customers reviews on Google. If you have ever done anything like this before, then you were moved by social proof.

Social proof is a powerful tool used frequently by sales professionals. Using the power of social proof alone can double and triple your sales. It can take your sales to a new level. The most successful products and services often use social proof because they know how effectively it affects consumer's psychology when it comes to making a buying decision.

Note this: 92% of people will trust a recommendation from a peer, and 70% of people will trust a recommendation from someone they don't even know *—Nielsen*

If others are buying it, then it must be good—that is how we usually think. If others are eating it, then it must be sweet. If others are going there, then it must be cool.

It is no longer a secret that humans are flawed when it comes to placing value on things. We often rely on so many factors or signs to determine whether the price or value placed on a good or service is worth it or not.

We look at how others react amongst other things to determine whether it is worth the price or not. A sales professional knows this, and he uses it to his advantage. He asks different customers for testimonials that focus on the most common customers' objections and carries them around as part of his sales tools.

Note that nine out of 10 people say they trust what a customer says about a business more than what that business says about itself. (Wyzowl)

Most times, when I go on a sales call and my prospective client objects, I show them one of my testimonials that answer their particular objection.

Start collecting testimonials. Start using your testimonials in all your sales calls from today. It is one of the most potent tools of a sales professional. And if you are a business owner, start using your testimonials in all your marketing activities.

This is why:

- 89% of marketers consider customer testimonials and case studies the most effective content forms for influencing purchases. —*Webdam*

- People trust your testimonials more than your advertising. A recent study shows that 83% of customers don't trust advertising. —*Status Labs*

- 88% of consumers trust online testimonials and reviews as much as recommendations from friends or family.—*Big Commerce*

- 97% of B2B customers cited testimonials and peer recommendations regarding the most reliable type of content.—*Demand Gen Report*

- Customer testimonials placed alongside more expensive items increased conversion rates by 380%. —*Power Reviews*

- Customer testimonials have the highest effectiveness rating for content marketing at 89%.—*Social Fresh*

- Regular use of testimonials can help you generate 62% more revenue from every customer, not just once but every time they visit your site. —*Big Commerce*

Using testimonials will help you build trust and credibility faster than you can ever do on your own.

However, please keep in mind that one format of testimonial(s) won't work for all your prospects because your prospects are all different!

Testimonials that show return on investment (ROI) for your customers work well for Assertive prospects. While testimonials where customers talk about how good your product or service is work well for other personality types like the Amiable, Expressive and Analytic prospects.

#21

THE LAW OF SOCIAL SELLING

More than 70% of Salespeople who use Social Media networking in their sales process outperform their peers who don't!

SOCIAL MEDIA POPULARITY AND REACH has exploded in an unprecedented fashion over the years. The rate at which organizations are generating leads through social media is unimaginable. The marketplace seems to have moved to social media platforms. Today, any business that neglects this fact does so at its peril.

The power of understanding and knowing your potential customers is now on the internet. Internet technology and social media have all presented sellers and buyers with unbelievable power and control. With few clicks of a button, a buyer and a seller can transact business that runs into millions of dollars without ever meeting physically or speaking over the phone. With over 75 billion devices connected to the internet, what goes on online is mind-blowing.

Check these impressive statistics:

- 67% of the buyer's journey is now done digitally (Sirius Decisions)

- 49% of users say they use Google to discover or find a new item or product. (Think with Google, 2019)

- There is an average of 100 billion monthly visitors on Google, with over 5.6 billion searches per day.

- 49% of consumers depend on influencer recommendations on social media.—*Oberlo*

- 73% of Marketers believe that social media marketing has been "somewhat effective" or "very effective for their business.—Oberlo

- *YouTube*: Almost 5 billion videos are watched on YouTube every single day; 6 out of 10 people prefer online video platforms to live TV.

- Of all the platforms, YouTube has the highest referral traffic rates. Over half of YouTubers use the site to learn how to do things they have never done before.

- More than 500 hours of videos are uploaded to YouTube every minute.

- *Instagram*: 75% of the Instagram audience is age 18 to 24. Over 90% of users follow at least one brand account; 67% of consumers are likely to spend more on a brand they follow; 78% of consumers say they will visit the physical retail store of a brand they follow and 84% of millennials are more likely to buy from a brand they follow.

Sellers are now presented with vast opportunities to sell their products and services without the need for a brick-and-mortar location.

With Google Display Ads, you can reach 90% of global internet users across more than three million websites and apps. This kind of reach allows you to learn about your customers' behaviour, identify valuables prospects and engage with them quickly and often.

The secret to what your customers or potential customers are looking for is hidden in their daily Google searches. The secret to understanding your potential customers is in their searches. The secret to understanding customer's behaviour and psychology can now be laid bare to whoever is willing to ask.

Every day, Google receives billions of search queries in the form of questions from your potential customers. Different questions—like how to, how can, where, what, when and why—are being asked every second.

Google Analytics can reveal some of these online behaviours of your potential customers. The Analytics can tell you how they landed on your website, the search query or the keyword that linked them to your site. It can tell you the pages they viewed while on your site and the actions they took. It can tell you where they spent most of their time on your site and what engages them.

With Analytics, you can view your customers' touchpoints with your brand; you can see data that tells you what attracts your customers and turns them off.

Other free online applications like *Similar Web* can reveal secrets of your competitor's social media marketing activities. With it, you can see the social media contents generating buzz for your competitors' products or services. You can know the platform that brings more leads and customers for them. Simply put, *Similar Web* can allow you to duplicate the success strategies of your best competitors.

With a few clicks, you can discover what others have spent millions of dollars to develop. Hey, the marketing strategies that were once a secret are no longer secret!

Google Keyword Planner can tell you the keywords your customers are searching for, helping you make better marketing decisions.

Your potential customers are now asking questions that they couldn't ask their grandmothers or anyone else. They are asking very personal questions, and they are seeking answers.

Buyers can now binge-watch Netflix on their sofas while buying things from any part of the world.

With just a few clicks of a button on Twitter, a mega business empire can crumble and tumble.

The power that businesses now have and the challenges they now face have never been bigger.

It is a blessing and a burden for all of us; anyhow, you want to interpret it.

Consider these facts:

- 1 out of 6 couples that married in the U.S in the 2019 year met online. (Source)

- 1 in 5 divorces is blamed on Facebook.

- More than 2.5 billion people are using Facebook.

Now, you are provided with an opportunity to know why. Why is my customer buying? Why is he not buying? Now you can know what motivates them to buy.

Now, you can track and understand their journey, where they are coming from and where they are going.

Recent research shows that 75% of companies that miss their revenue goals don't know their visitor, lead, qualified leads, or sales opportunities data. For a company or salesman that harnesses the power of internet technology and social media, this should no longer be a problem.

What we now know:

- Twitter says 80% of their advertisers' inbound social customer service requests happen on Twitter.

- 81% of U.S. online consumers' purchase decisions are influenced by their friend's social media posts.

- 84% of CEOs and VPs use social media to make purchasing decisions (Source IDC)

A caveat: There is such a thing as a social media crisis.

Companies and social media professionals need to be prepared for times when something might go wrong. Have a plan in place on what to do before, during and after a social media crisis. It can save your organization from total collapse.

Develop and create a social media policy. Remember Murphy's Law: *"Anything that can go wrong will go wrong."*

The law is valid with social media.

#22

THE LAW OF MARKET DEVELOPMENT

"If you want to master winning more –new sales, it requires mastering creating new opportunities." —**Mike Weinberg, Consultant & Sales Expert**

THERE IS A COLD TRUTH YOU NEED TO GET USED TO. Whatever you think you have as a competitive advantage over others will soon be lost to someone else, and that is if it is not already lost.

One of the largest business corporations, IBM, popularly referred to as the "Big Blue," can testify to this fact. The Big Blue once dominated the computing world in both hardware and software and never imagined that a time was coming when smaller, lesser players would supplant it.

For decades, the company had been so successful that everyone was stunned when they declared quarterly losses of $8bn in 1993, caused by increased competition and changing market. The price of IBM mainframe computers dropped by 90%, and Big Blue lost money and lost its market share. Guess who became the market leaders? HP, Dell, and Apple, the new competitors—companies that could best be described as "Big Blue's great-grandchildren".

Know this: Nothing will ever guarantee your position in the market. If giant corporations like IBM and Kodak could be busted, if these behemoths could lose their market share and lose their money despite their size, their technical know-how and management mastery, then you too can lose your competitive edge.

In truth, you can wake up one day to find your whole business wiped out. Nothing is more certain in the marketplace like change. This is the hard reality of the market.

What can you do as a salesman or a business owner to ensure that you are not wiped out? The answer is always to try to develop new markets. You must create a blue ocean outside of your current red ocean to continue to swim without hindrance.

Chan Kim and Renee Mauborgne, in their book *Blue Ocean Strategy*, described blue oceans as all the industries not in existence today. *The unknown market spaces.*

The current market is regarded as the "Red Ocean" because companies try to outperform each other to gain greater market share. The red ocean market is crowded; prospects for profit and growth are reduced. Products in the red ocean soon become commodities, and cutthroat competition makes the red ocean bloody.

Hence, the red ocean is not where you want to be. Think about it, the current red ocean where you find yourself today was somebody else's initial blue ocean. Eventually, every blue ocean becomes a red ocean, but if you are the one that created the blue ocean, you would have made all your profit before the ocean turns red. You will be the first in the mind of consumers. Remember the first law in *"The 22 Immutable Laws of Marketing"* by Al Ries and Jack Trout: *It is better to be the first than it is to be better.*

To create a blue ocean (new market), Kim and Mauborgne raised four questions you need to answer:

- Which of the factors regarding your product or service are taken for granted within your industry that should be eliminated?

- Which factors as regards your product or service should be reduced well below the industry's standard?

- Regarding your product or service, which factors should be raised well above the industry's standard?

- Which factors as regards your product or service should be created that the industry has never offered?

One company that answered these questions brilliantly was Southwest Airlines. Joe Brancatelli sums it up well in his online article "Southwest Airlines' Seven Secrets of Success."

One-Plane Fits All

Unlike the network carriers and their commuter surrogates, which operate all manner of regional jets, turboprops, narrow-body and wide-body aircraft, Southwest flies just one plane type, the Boeing 737 series. It saves Southwest millions in maintenance costs—spare-parts inventories, mechanic training, and other nuts-and-bolts airline issues. It also gives the airline unique flexibility to move its 527 aircraft throughout the route network without costly disruptions and reconfigurations.

Point-To-Point Flying

Network carriers rely on a hub-and-spoke system, which laboriously collects passengers from "spoke" cities, flies them to a central "hub" airport, and redistributes them to other spokes. Not Southwest. Most of its flying is non-stop between two points. That minimizes the time that planes sit on the ground at crowded, delay-prone hubs and allows the average Southwest aircraft to be in the air for more than an hour longer each day than a similarly sized jet flown by a network carrier. Southwest's avoid-the-hubs strategy also pays dividends in on-time operations. According to Flight Stats, Southwest's 78 per cent on-time performance in June is eight percentage points higher than the industry average and higher than that of any of its major competitors.

Simple In-Flight Service

Business travellers haven't always loved Southwest's über-simple service, but it's looking better and better as competitors cut back. There is just one service class, a decent coach cabin that is slightly more spacious than those of Southwest's competitors. There are no assigned seats. There have never been meals, just beverages and snacks. Keeping it basic allows Southwest to unload a flight, clean and restock the plane, and board another flight full of passengers in as little as 20 minutes compared with as much as 90 minutes on a network airline. Airline efficiency experts say that the savings allow each Southwest jet to fly an extra flight per day. Extra flights mean extra revenue.

No Frills, No Fees

As other carriers have rushed to remove perks and pile on fees and restrictions, Southwest has kept its customer proposition streamlined and transparent. The airline only sells one-way fares and only in a few price "buckets." That not only keeps costs down—complex fare structures are expensive to manage—it convinces fliers that they are getting value for money. Prices are all-inclusive too. Southwest doesn't have fuel surcharges, doesn't charge for standby travel or ticket changes, and continues to permit travellers to check two pieces of luggage free. And since every seat on every flight is virtually identical, passengers know precisely what they will get when purchasing.

Look at what everybody within your industry is doing and locate questions begging to be asked. What is it that they are doing that is not adding value to your customers? Perhaps it adds value, but the value is so negligible that customers can do without it. Is there something more valuable to the customer that your industry is not considering? How can you provide more of this value to your customers? And what value do you think your customers will find valuable that your industry is not providing yet?

Other questions you can ask to open up a new market are:

- *Can we reduce the complexity of our product and service so that it will be easier for our customers to use?*

That was the question that Casella Wines answered that created a multi-million-dollar blue ocean market for them. They found that wine retailers in the United States offered buyers aisles of wine varieties, but to the general consumer, the choice was overwhelming. The bottles looked the same, and labels were complicated with enological terminology understood only by wine connoisseurs. The choice was so extensive that sales clerks at retail shops were at an equal disadvantage in understanding or recommending wine to bewildered potential buyers.

Casella changed all that by creating ease of selection. It reduced the range of wines offered, creating only two: Chardonnay, the most popular white in the United States and a red, Shiraz. It removed all technical jargon from the bottles and created a straightforward and non-traditional label (Kim & Mauborgne, 2005). The result of this move was an unprecedented success for Casella, worth billions of dollars.

- *What would have to happen for your customers to need your product or service?*

- *What is your customer trying to achieve by using your product or service?*

Nearly 97% of your competitors are neither asking these questions nor trying to answer them. Answering some of these questions is your Holy Grail to create your blue ocean!

The development of new markets is the future of every business. Someone somewhere will always find a way to sell what you are selling at a lower price, deliver it faster, and produce it at a higher quality.

#23

THE LAW OF CONTRAST

"The most successful businesses are the ones that have been able to differentiate themselves the most from others."

—Professor William K. Hall

HOW DO YOU SEPARATE YOUR PRODUCT FROM THE REST? If you cannot differentiate your product, you cannot sell. Your competitive advantage lies in your differentiation. Your products and services' ability to fulfil their true potential depends on how well you create contrast between them and other similar products or services within your market. It is one of the biggest challenges that every marketer and sales professional face.

When you meet prospective customers, the first set of words they want to hear from your mouth is how your product or service is different from others, why they should buy from you, and what makes you special. There are so many me-too products and services around. The most successful businesses are the ones that have been able to differentiate themselves the most from others.

How does the brain cope with the huge amount of information around us and select where and what to focus on? It uses some elimination and selection rules known as cognitive biases. Humans have over 188 different cognitive biases, which forms the rules by which we make our decisions. To know all the cognitive biases might be a challenge. The good news is that these 188 rules of making decisions are triggered by six elements.

As we already know, the primal brain plays a vital role in decision making, and these same six elements act as stimulants for the primal brain. This understanding is the foundation of Neuromarketing.

But because of our focus, I will explain the first two elements that will allow you to create the much-needed contrast for your product or service.

Two Elements to create massive Contrast

1. Personal

2. Contrastable

Personal

To stimulate your prospective customers' primal brain and influence them to pick your product over others, you need to make it about them; thus, the word personal. Stop talking about yourself and start talking about them. Stop using the word "WE" and start using the word "YOU". People don't care about what you know until they know how much you care.

When you look everywhere, from social media to websites to marketing and sales materials, you see organisations talking about themselves rather than about their customers. You see things like "What WE Do! Who WE Are! About Us!"

If your wish is to persuade your audience to buy from you, then you must put the spotlight back on them. It would be best to recognise that your prospects are the stars of the show because the primal brain is primarily focused on survival, which made us fundamentally selfish as individuals. Hence, the reason we are always more interested in things that focus on us rather than others. The legendary evolutionary biologist Richard Dawkins believes that our selfishness goes down to our genes. Have you noticed how we tend to look more at ourselves even in a group photograph? And no matter how many times you have seen the group photograph, you always spend more time looking at yourself than others.

How do we, as salespeople and marketers, think that we can persuade others by focusing on ourselves rather than on them?

Contrastable

To get the primal brain's attention, you need to introduce something to it that is different from its present condition. What do I mean by this? If you want to get anybody's attention in a quiet place, you can introduce a loud noise! This sort of variation from the norm is what gets the attention of the primal brain.

As a salesman or a marketer, to get your target audience's attention, you need to stop saying what other salespeople and marketers are saying and start saying something different. Guess what others are saying? "Who We Are! Our product is the best available. Our product is the cheapest…"

Instead, start saying things like, "Why this product is for YOU! How this product will transform YOU! Why this service is perfect for YOUR business."

Notice the differences in the messages. While the first set put the spotlight on the seller (celebrating themselves on their own show and channel), the second set of messages put the spotlight on the customers (celebrating them as the star on the show).

However, you must be creative in how you create contrast for your products and services. First, know what others are doing, then do the opposite. In Africa's most populous nation Nigeria, the first and foreign mobile network was MTN with its distinctive Yellow colour and the famous "Y'ello Nigeria" tagline. MTN became remarkably successful with millions of subscribers across the country. Then came another mobile network operator, and guess what, its colour was Red! And it became a roaring success too. And finally, an indigenous mobile network operator came into the picture by the name Globacom. And it chose to be Green! It was no surprise that it also became a roaring success, wooing Nigeria's citizens with the "Glo Naija" slogan.

Seeing the successes of these mobile operators, another operator came into the scene. And the result: *BusinessDay Weekender* in May 2020 reported that the mobile network failed to record growth in internet users for nearly four years, and it had less than 7% of the voice market in Nigeria. Do you want to guess its colour? The answer is Green! The mobile network was later sold, and the new owners changed its name.

When you fail to create contrast with your competition, when all you do is create me-too products or messages, your sales suffer! But if you can find a way to differentiate your product or service from your competitors and do it well, you will become a success.

HERE IS AN INSIGHT SHARED BY DAVID OGILVY in *Ogilvy On Advertising*: "In a *Harvard Business Review* article, Professor William K. Hall reported on a study of eight industries, from steel to beer. The most successful companies were those that best differentiated their products.

What makes you different is what makes you unique. It is your identity. It is the reason prospective clients would do business with you.

There are lots of ways through which you can create contrast. You can do this by being more caring and more committed to providing your customers with more value than your competitors.

You can create contrast by always choosing to do more than you are paid for, even if your product is entirely the same as that of your competitors. You can choose to serve your customers more than they are expecting you to do.

Napoleon Hill, in his book, *The Law of Success*, shared a story that captured this well. "A customer purchased an expensive lace waist at the Field store but did not wear it. Two years later she gave it to her niece as a wedding present. The niece quietly returned the lace waist to the Field store and exchanged it for other merchandise. Even though it had been out for more than two years and was then out of style. Not only did the Field store take back the lace waist, but what is of more importance is that it did so without argument!

The woman who returned the lace waist knew she was not entitled to a rebate; therefore, when the store gave her that to which she was not entitled, the transaction won her as a permanent customer.

But the transaction's effect did not end there; it only began, for this woman spread the news of the fair treatment she had received at the Field store, far and near. It was the talk of the women of her set for many days, and the Field store received more advertising from the transaction than it could have purchased in any other way with ten times the value of the lace waist."

This story more than explained what I had in mind regarding creating a contrast between you and your competitors. The truth is you might not always be able to compete based on price or quality, but you can indeed find other ways to do more for your customers if you are willing.

You can truly separate yourself from others when you form the habit of doing more than your customer expects from you. That is when you can give your product or service the real identity. And it is not too difficult to bring a different touch to a sales situation. Remember, we are all human, and we all like to be treated like one, with dignity and respect.

When I graduated from university, I started an interior decoration company with my brother. The first client we had was pissed at our job. I could ask my brother, the operations manager, to sort out the problem. Instead, I decided to go with him and the workers to do the job again and, second, to apologize personally to the customer. When we got there and introduced myself as the company's Chief Executive Officer to the client, she was surprised. "You could have sent your guys," she said. Yes. "But I needed to come and apologize for the poor service personally," I told her.

Before I left, the news was everywhere. *Oh, the chief executive came to apologize and supervise my work personally.* To cut the story short, we left the place with ten new orders. And that formed the foundation of our customer base on which we built the entire business.

In their book, rapper 50 Cent and Robert Greene, The 50th Law said, your power is in who you are. Some people try to be like others. Hence, they lose their uniqueness and their power. What makes you different is your uniqueness. Your uniqueness is your power. In your power is your DNA.

Know the habits of those who fail in sales and avoid those things like the plagues. Don't sell as they sell. Don't talk like they talk. Don't read what they read. Know their language but don't speak it. Embrace your uniqueness because that is your power. Don't be a conformist. When you conform, you lose your power and your edge.

Be different and sell differently!

About the author

Joshua Riches is the CEO and Senior Sales Consultant of Sales Mafia. He has trained numerous salespeople and organisations on acquiring more customers and selling more of their products and services.

He is an associate member of the Chartered Institute of Marketing in the United Kingdom and Microsoft Advertising Certified Professional. He has degrees in Computer Science, Economics, Managerial Psychology and Marketing.

He has over 20 years of experience in Sales, Marketing and Business Development and over 30 certifications in Sales, Marketing and Digital Advertising from Google, Facebook, Amazon, and HubSpot Academy.

www.ingramcontent.com/pod-product-compliance
Lightning Source LLC
Chambersburg PA
CBHW071207220526
45468CB00002B/528